RAGE AGAINST JIHAD
The Revenge
A novel by
James Earl Gaylord
© 2017

The wife, daughter, son and five grandchildren of the central

character, Jamie, are killed in a nuclear bomb detonated by

terrorists in Chicago, Illinois. Jamie is 65 and, very quietly,

one of the wealthiest men in the world. He made his wealth

as a computer scientist and owns many companies providing

computer security services to governments and businesses all

over the world. One of his companies provides computer

security services to the House of Saud and to many members

of the House of bin Laden. Jamie has managed to become

very rich without coming to the attention of the media. He is,

as far as the world is concerned, a nonentity.

This novel is about Jamie and his family and how he came to

be in a position to find and punish those he believes

responsible for the murders of his family. The story of his life and how and against whom he takes his revenge ranges from a college town in the Midwestern US in the 1940's, to Graceland subdivision in Memphis in the 1950's, Vietnam in 1966, Memphis in 1968, radical student politics and the sanitation worker's strike which brought Martin Luther King to his death on 4 April 1968, New York City in 1969, England in 1970 and in the dramatic conclusion, Saudi Arabia, England. It ties together Islam, information technology, computer science, satellite controlled drones, global positioning, DNA, nanotechnology, world government, terrorism, international banking and exotic weapons. The cast of characters includes Jamie and five of his closest associates, the House of Saud, the House of bin Laden, Free Masonry, the Muslim Brotherhood and a British Lord. The period covered is from 1940 to 2020.

This novel is written to engage and entertain readers. It is fiction.

.

Jihad-"Fatwa"

From the web site

http://www.fas.org/irp/world/para/docs/980223-fatwa.htm:

The following statement from Usama bin Laden and his associates purports to be a religious ruling (fatwa) requiring the killing of Americans, both civilian and military. This document is part of the evidence that links the bin Laden network to the September 11,2001 terrorist attacks on New **York and Washington. "**

"Jihad Against Jews and Crusaders

World Islamic Front Statement

23 February 1998

"The Arabian Peninsula has never -- since Allah made it flat, created its desert, and encircled it with seas -- been stormed by any forces like the crusader armies spreading in it like locusts, eating its riches and wiping out its plantations. All this is happening at a time in which

nations are attacking Muslims like people fighting over a plate of food. In the light of the grave situation and the lack of support, we and you are obliged to discuss current events, and we should all agree on how to settle the matter.

No one argues today about three facts that are known to everyone; we will list them, in order to remind everyone: First, for over seven years the United States has been occupying the lands of Islam in the holiest of places, the Arabian Peninsula, plundering its riches, dictating to its rulers, humiliating its people, terrorizing its neighbors, and turning its bases in the Peninsula into a spearhead through which to fight the neighboring Muslim peoples. If some people have in the past argued about the fact of the occupation, all the people of the Peninsula have now acknowledged it. The best proof of this is the Americans' continuing aggression against the Iraqi people using the Peninsula as a staging post, even though all its rulers are against their territories being used to that end, but they are helpless.

Second, despite the great devastation inflicted on the Iraqi people by the crusader-Zionist alliance, and despite the huge number of those killed, which has exceeded 1 million... despite all this, the Americans are once against trying to repeat the horrific massacres, as though they are not content with the protracted blockade imposed after the ferocious war or the fragmentation and devastation. So here they come to annihilate what is left of this people and to humiliate their Muslim neighbors.

Third, if the Americans' aims behind these wars are religious and economic, the aim is also to serve the Jews' petty state and divert attention from its occupation of Jerusalem and murder of Muslims there. The best proof of this is their eagerness to destroy Iraq, the strongest neighboring Arab state, and their endeavor to fragment all the states of the region such as Iraq, Saudi Arabia, Egypt, and Sudan into paper statelets and through their disunion and weakness to guarantee Israel's survival and the continuation of the brutal crusade occupation of the Peninsula.

All these crimes and sins committed by the Americans are a clear declaration of war on Allah, his messenger, and Muslims. And ulema have throughout Islamic history unanimously agreed that the jihad is an individual duty if the enemy destroys the Muslim countries. This was revealed by Imam Bin-Qadamah in "Al- Mughni," Imam al-Kisa'i in "Al-Bada'i," al-Qurtubi in his interpretation, and the shaykh of al-Islam in his books, where he said: "As for the fighting to repulse [an enemy], it is aimed at defending sanctity and religion, and it is a duty as agreed [by the ulema]. Nothing is more sacred than belief except repulsing an enemy who is attacking religion and life." On that basis, and in compliance with Allah's order, we issue the following fatwa to all Muslims:

The ruling to kill the Americans and their allies -- civilians and military -- is an individual duty for every Muslim who can do it in any country in which it is possible to do it, in order to liberate the al-Aqsa Mosque and the holy mosque [Mecca] from their grip, and in order for their armies to move out of all the lands of Islam, defeated and unable to threaten any Muslim. This is in accordance with the words of Almighty Allah, "and fight the pagans all together as they fight you all together," and "fight them until there is no more tumult or oppression, and there prevail justice and faith in Allah."

This is in addition to the words of Almighty Allah: "And why should ye not fight in the cause of Allah and of those who, being weak, are ill-treated (and oppressed)? --

women and children, whose cry is: 'Our Lord, rescue us from this town, whose people are oppressors; and raise for us from thee one who will help!'"

We -- with Allah's help -- call on every Muslim who believes in Allah and wishes to be rewarded to comply with Allah's order to kill the Americans and plunder their money wherever and whenever they find it. We also call on Muslim ulema, leaders, youths, and soldiers to launch the raid on Satan's U.S. troops and the devil's supporters allying with them, and to displace those who are behind them so that they may learn a lesson.

Almighty Allah said: "O ye who believe, give your response to Allah and His Apostle, when He calleth you to that which will give you life. And know that Allah cometh between a man and his heart, and that it is He to whom ye shall all be gathered."

Almighty Allah also says: "O ye who believe, what is the matter with you, that when ye are asked to go forth in the cause of Allah, ye cling so heavily to the earth! Do ye prefer the life of this world to the hereafter? But little is the comfort of this life, as compared with the hereafter. Unless ye go forth, He will punish you with a grievous penalty, and put others in your place; but Him ye would not harm in the least. For Allah hath power over all things."

Almighty Allah also says: "So lose no heart, nor fall into despair. For ye must gain mastery if ye are true in faith."

This is a work of fiction which uses some real events

On September 11, 2001, the largest attack against the United States in history was carried out by a group of terrorists claiming to be followers of Islam. Three plane loads of men, women and children, were vaporized as their civilian airplanes hit the World Trade Center in New York City and the Pentagon in Arlington, Virginia. A fourth flight crashed into a field in Pennsylvania as it was headed to another target. This set in motion events which would change the world.

Some years later elements of the same group which planned and carried out the September 11, 2001 massacre successfully detonated a nuclear weapon in Chicago, Illinois which killed more than 400,000 more people. Among those killed were the wife, daughter, son and three grandchildren of Jamie McWhitt, one of the richest men in the world. At the age of 65, Jamie was in China on a business trip when the bomb was detonated in Chicago. He learned almost immediately about the death of his family. The pain he felt numbed him but his pain was quickly replaced by anger. He had watched as the U.S government tried to track down and destroy those responsible for the 9/11/01 and Chicago attacks. The US government had spent billions of dollars to find and destroy those who had carried out the attacks. It had managed to finally kill Osama bin Laden in his hideout in Pakistan. Nevertheless the Islamists who sought to destroy the US had grown in numbers which eventually led them to the deadly attack on

Chicago. This time, however, it would be Jamie who would seek and destroy those who had murdered his family. Jamie vowed he would have revenge regardless of how long it would take and regardless of what he would have to do.

Chapter One- Religion

Jamie was not a religious man. Until he was 16 years old he had attended Sunday school and Church at a Methodist Church every Sunday with his parents. After his 16th birthday his parents allowed him to decide if he wanted to continue to attend religious services. By that time Jamie had decided that religion was evil and that it was the root cause of many of the problems of the world. Later in his life he particularly liked the wording of the song "Imagine" and its reference to a world which was not divided by religion. He never went to Church again except to attend funerals or weddings. During his life he had gained an active dislike for many religions. Islam to Jamie was a particularly evil religion whose many adherents thought nothing of killing innocent people. Islam was divided into hundreds of sects many of whom often killed members of sects different than their own. To Jamie the expression which best summed up Islam was the one that many Moslems used concerning non-Moslems- "Death to the Infidels". He also understood the many evils done throughout history in the name of Christianity. Jamie had managed to live his life while following many of the ideals expressed by religions. He believed in the Golden Rule and had managed to live his life without killing another human being. In his life he had always sought to be honest and charitable and to tolerate those who were different than himself. He respected other cultures and those whose views of life were different than his own.

Chapter Two-Jamie's Mask

Jamie's face served as a mask which hid the anger which burned deep in his mind and heart like a searing brand on the rump of a branded calf. He awoke each morning with his anger serving in place of a morning cup of coffee. Anger, of course, is not an uncommon emotion. Webster's defines "anger" as a "feeling of great displeasure, hostility, indignation, or exasperation- "wrath". Jamie's anger was not mere displeasure. It had surely become "rage" which Webster's defines as "violent anger, burning desire or passion". This was true. Jamie's anger burned passionately within him. Now every minute of his day was driven by his anger. Jamie was going to have his revenge. Jamie had a plan. His search for those responsible for the deaths of his family, had taken him to Saudi Arabia where he believed he would find those against whom he would take his revenge.

From age eight, spurred on by a next door neighbor, Jamie had been interested in what would become computer science. His neighbor at that time was a professor of electrical engineering at the University of Illinois and a prolific inventor. The Professor grew to view Jamie as the son he had never had and from age 8 to 13 Jamie hung around the Professor's basement laboratory and read the many books and research papers recommended to him by the Professor. At age ten Jamie had followed the writings of Vannevar Bush and other innovators who outlined many of the principals which would lay the foundation for the Internet.

Jamie's interest in computer science continued after his family moved away from Illinois. At the age of 16 Jamie taught himself the computer programming language known as FORTRAN and as the years went by Jamie learned COBOL and ADA and all he could learn about computers. To Jamie the computer was a giant library capable of storing the knowledge of the world as fast as it was created. He viewed the computer as the means to make the world a better place by providing easier access to knowledge. Jamie also knew that the computer could be an awesome weapon.

Chapter Three- Who Did It?

Jamie believed that he would find the answer to the question he had asked himself when his family was murdered.. Who did it?

Jamie focused his research on two Saudi families. The House of bin Laden and the House of Saud and the more research he did the more he became convinced that the House of bin Laden served the House of Saud.

Now he wanted to find out who the House of Saud served.

Jamie owned a company, one of many, which provided computer and internet services to the House of Saud and to the House of bin Laden. His company had worked for the House of Saud for a dozen years and employed more than 200 Saudi including several members of the House of Saud. Through his company Jamie could see the many data bases in which members of the House of Saud stored correspondence, notes, memos, emails, etc. He had all of the passwords to all of the secrets various members of the House of Saud had committed to their computers. Most of what was in the data bases was in Arabic but some was in English and some was in French. The sheer volume of the information was stupendous.

The House of Saud, a hereditary monarchy, had grown to number more than

30,000 people. Although the House of Saud is an ancient family it was unified into its modern form by King Abdul Aziz bin Abdul Rahman al-Saud, usually known by his shorter name of Ibn Saud. The House of Saud gave its' name to the Country of Saudi Arabia when Ibn Saud declared himself King of Saudi Arabia, in 1932, the year Saudi Arabia came into existence as an independent country. For more than 200 years the House of Saud has followed the strict Wahhabi Moslem sect. In 1744, an earlier House of Saud ruler, had married one of his sons to the daughter of the Moslem cleric who had founded Wahhabism, a sect whose adherents believed they were gods' chosen people. Saudi Arabia would have remained a small, primitive desert nation had it not been for the discovery of vast fields of oil in 1938. Since the discovery of oil the House of Saud had used its' oil wealth to strengthen its control of the country.

Much of the oil wealth has been squandered to permit favored members of the House of Saud to lead very extravagant life styles. By September 11, 2001, the House of Saud had invested more than two trillion dollars in the United States in stocks, bonds, certificates of deposit and real estate. This gave them the ability to greatly influence U.S. foreign policy concerning the Saudis. In particular it led U.S. politicians to ignore the growing signs of Saudi hostility towards the U.S. The Saudis also had huge investments in Europe and many of the Saudi Princes in the House of Saud maintained palatial estates in Europe at which they could lead a life style which would have been prohibited in Saudi Arabia. Many members of the House of Saud led dual existences. One as followers of their strict version of Islam and the other as Playboys of the Western world. Like any large family real power in the house of Saud was in the hands of a small number of family members beginning with seven of the sons of King Ibn Saud. However, even the central leadership core had to satisfy the greater family. Otherwise they could not rule. Satisfying the divergent views of the members of the House of Saud required many compromises. It sometimes meant that the official views of the House of Saud would be to take both sides of an issue. It meant that a criminal might be found innocent but still have his / her head chopped off. It was safer to give each faction in the family something to keep them happy. Let some elements of the family attack and kill Westerners but at the same time chop off a few Saudis heads as a fake gesture of opposition to the murders. During his lifetime King Ibn Saud decreed, through the Saudi constitution, that the King of Saudi Arabia had to be one of his sons. He was known to have at least 37 sons by his many wives's but seven of these sons were particularly favored. These seven sons formed the core of the House of Saud and ruled the country with an iron fist. During the 1970's the House of Saud began using its vast fortune to spread the fundamentals of Wahhabism all over the world by forming and financing religious schools. These religious schools offered educations to the sons of poor Moslem families. Many of these religious schools were set up in Pakistan and in Afghanistan. From the religious schools in Afghanistan came the Taliban rulers of that country. One of the foremost political philosophers supported by the House of Saud was a member of the House of bin Laden, Osama bin Laden. It was felt that Osama bin Laden would attract too much attention to the House of Saud and to Saudi Arabia and so Sudan and than Afghanistan became the base of operations for bin Laden. To be able to let families know when their sons had enlisted in endeavors led by bin Laden he began keeping a base register of all those who came to his cause. This base (Al Qaeda) gave the organization its' name.

In all of the religious schools sponsored by the House of Saud the principals of Wahhabism dominated. The Wahhabis believe that they are God's chosen people and that all other Moslems and all the rest of the world were infidels to be converted or killed. The House of Saud rules Saudi Arabia according to the laws of Islam as interpreted by Wahhabi. Under the Rule of the Wahhabis, like in Afghanistan under the Taliban, women lived as vassals to men. The sole role of women in a Wahhabi household was to bear and raise children. Outside of the home Wahhabi keeps women hidden from view with robes and veils. Saudi men are expected to follow the Wahhabi view of Islamic law and can be severely punished for drinking alcohol or public infidelity. Many male members of the House of Saud lead dual lives. Once they leave Saudi Arabia they violate every element of Islamic law. They drink, gamble, worship extravagance and actively and openly cavort with women in a non Islamic fashion. Foremost, the Wahhabis, in their religious schools, taught hatred of the West in general and the United States in particular. Even religious schools founded in the United States to teach American Moslems, taught hatred of the United States. Jamie quickly learned that every single one of the 9/11 hijackers had been educated in the religious schools operated by the Saudis.

The House of bin Laden, unlike the House of Saud came from humble origins. The prosperity and prominence of the bin Ladens began with Muhammad bin Oud bin Laden. It was said that he descended from Yemini slaves or at the best from Yemini laborers. Although Muhammad bin

Laden was not an educated man he was said to have a mind like a computer and was a talented engineer. In the 1950's bin Laden won the favor of King Saud, who was confined to a wheelchair, by building him a ramp so he could be pushed up to the second floor of his palace. It was also said that he had build a remarkable road which shortened the Royal Families commute to their summer palace in the coolness of the mountains of At Taif. Legend said that in 1964 King Faisal, who had succeeded his father, King Saud upon King Saud's death, thanked Muhammad by giving him the contract to build a network of roads in the country. In 1973 the House of Saud gave the bin Laden family a contract to rebuild the Islamic holy sites at Mecca and Medina. This project is said to have earned the bin Ladens more than 20 billion dollars. After many hours of research and review of many contradictory reports Jamie concluded that the relationship between Osama bin Laden and the House of Saud was much like that between a drug kingpin and a trusted Lt.

After two months of intense study Jamie called together his five closest friends, and asked for their help. He asked that they choose a trusted subordinate to take over the daily management of their companies and to move with him to Saudi Arabia. He explained to them what he wanted to do. He wanted to find out who had planned, financed and managed the attacks on America. After leaving Illinois Jamie and his five friends met in England in a country estate in Southern England near the legendary town of Winchester. Jamie hired a staff of Saudi expatriates to teach Jamie and his friends how to read, speak and write Arabic. For six intense months the six men spent ten hours a day, six days a week learning to be Saudis. They were totally immersed in Saudi language and culture. They ate Saudi food, they watched Saudi television and they learned to speak and write Arabic. Jamie had the men divided into five different groups and the Arabic they were learning was taught by Saudi expatriates from four Saudi cities- Jeddah, Taif, Najara and Riyadh. Although Arabic is the common language of Saudi Arabia like any language it varies slightly depending upon the tribal culture which dominates a particular area. After six months in England the six men took up residence in four different areas of Saudi Arabia. Jamie was in Jeddah. John Devore and George Thornton in Taif, Dave Mandrake in Najara, Bill Morgan and Weldon Roberts in Riyadh.

In the last fifty years, with its immense oil wealth, the population of Saudi Arabia had increased from 3 million to about 20 million people and the country continued to have one of the highest birth rates in the world. In addition the oil wealth of the Saudis had made them lazy and more than five million guest workers from all over the world had come to Saudi to do the jobs the Saudis didn't want to do. Almost all manual labor in Saudi Arabia was performed by people from other countries. From Egypt, Jordan, Indonesia, the Philippines, Thailand and Africa came people willing to collect garbage, clean streets, houses and businesses. From all over the world guest workers came to Saudi Arabia to do the jobs the Saudis were too lazy to do. Manual laborers, technicians, engineers, doctors, dentists. Many of these guest workers were exploited and mistreated by their Saudi employers and many of them were punished for violations of Islamic law. These punishments could include public execution or long sentences in Saudi prisons..

Jeddah is the second largest city in Saudi Arabia with more than a million and a half people and lies along the coast of the Red Sea. It is often called the Paris of Arabia. At one time it had been the site of what was said to be the tomb of Eve. However, as the Wahhabis came, more and more, to control religious thought in Saudi Arabia the tomb was destroyed as being a perversion to Islam. The Taliban was to do much the same in Afghanistan when they destroyed the giant statues of Buddha.

The house in Jeddah was built into a small hill which afforded Jamie a broad view of the city. After reviewing the particulars of many Saudis, Jamie hired a Saudi who went by the name of Mustafa. Mustafa came from a Bedouin background but had been educated in Germany. He spoke fluent Arabic with a Saudi accent. He, like almost all Saudis, was a Moslem but from what Jamie could determine Mustafa may have been a Moslem only because Saudis were required to follow Islamic law and failure to do so could be dangerous. The Bedouin tribe from which Mustafa had come had almost completely

disappeared into urban areas of Saudi Arabia. Many

Bedouins felt estranged from the Saudi government

and it was clear to Jamie that Mustafa had no love for

the House of Saud. He was later to learn that two of

Mustafa's brothers had been executed by the House of

Saud after a 1979 uprising during which Islamic radicals

had seized Mecca. The House of Saud was able to re-

take Mecca using plans of Mecca provided by the bin

Ladens. For many years the Saudi government had

been trying to integrate Bedouins into Saudi society.

The Bedouin Moslems didn't fit the Saudi view of what

a Moslem should be. The singing and dancing which

many Bedouins performed as part of their religion didn't

fit the Wahhabi view of the Qur'an.

 Mustafa had met a German woman while he was in

Germany and she had become a Moslem in order to

marry Mustafa and live in

Saudi Arabia. Unlike most German women she had dark features and could easily pass for a Moslem when she went to the Market.

Jamie hired Mustafa to teach him more about Jeddah, Bedouins and Saudi Arabia.. By the time he arrived in Jeddah Jamie spoke nearly flawless Arabic and could read and write the language as well or better than most Saudis. Jamie, although he had pale skin, could pass for a Saudi. The years had turned his red hair to white and he wore contact lenses which made his blue eyes look brown. He wore the same sort of clothing that most Saudi men wore. He would wear a thawb (ankle length shirt) and a ghutra (head dress) He could go out into the streets in Saudi Arabia and blend in with the crowd. In addition to learning to speak and write the language Jamie studied the mannerisms of the Saudis. He also learned how to tell what region of the country a Saudi man might come from. Mustafa enjoyed taking Jamie to meet Bedouin tribe members and Jamie enjoyed these visits during which he would sit cross legged on a fine rug and drink tea with Bedouin elders. Mustafa explained to Jamie what united Saudis and what divided them. As part of his daily routine Jamie would pray in the direction of Mecca five times a day. Mustafa found this amusing. His own prayers, when in private, were short and not very earnest. Jamie's silent daily prayers gave Jamie a few moments to gather his thoughts of the moment. Although his prayers were towards Mecca it was not to Allah that Jamie prayed.

Jamie had many conversations with Mustafa in Arabic and it became apparent that Mustafa was not a fan of the House of Saud. In fact, like many Saudis Mustafa hated the House of Saud. Also, like most Saudis, he was careful to keep this hatred to himself.

When he had hired Mustafa Jamie had told him that he was a scholar and that he was writing a book about Jeddah. Jamie had never told Mustafa what nationality he was and Mustafa never asked. Jamie's house in Jeddah was a nice home but it was not a palace. It was a home befitting a scholar and not one which would distinguish Jamie as one of the wealthiest men in the world

John Devore settled in a house in Western Saudi Arabia in Taif which is the Summer Capitol for much of Saudi's elite. It is a beautiful resort area in the mountains above Mecca and is known for its' beautiful gardens and trees. It is more than 2000 feet above sea level and unlike most of Saudi Arabia has a cooler climate during the hot Saudi summers. The house in which John Devore settled was on a mountain road overlooking Taif and Mecca. From the house he could see the holy sites of

Mecca. He had brought with him an Englishman who, in the spirit of Lawrence of Arabia, was a life long devotee of Saudi Arabia. By this time John Devore had nearly mastered Arabic even though he still had a slight accent. He could read and write the language and was able to follow the events of the city of Taif by listening to radio and watching local television. He could easily pass for a Saudi and went to the local Mosque five times daily for prayers and to listen to the Sermons and pronouncements of the local Imam. Most of his prayers were silent prayers that Navy beat Army in the sport of the season. In reality John was a Southern Baptist.

Dave Mandrake and George Thornton settled in the city of Najara in the southwestern part of Saudi Arabia. Najara had a reputation as being the most modern city in Saudi Arabia. It also was said to be an important route for smugglers. Najara didn't fit the image most Americans had of Saudi Arabia. It contained many trees and orchards and in the vast deserts of Saudi Arabia was an oasis of beauty.

Bill Morgan and Weldon Roberts settled in the capital city of Riyadh and were able to fit in without much notice among the four million people in the Saudi capital.

Before leaving England the six men had met and Jamie had outlined what he wanted to do. He told the men that the attacks on the US were the start of a complex war being fought all over the world. He told the men that he knew that in any war they would find one person who led that war. It was Jamie's intention to track down that one person and kill that person. Any war leader has important key followers who helped the leader wage war. Jamie intended to find out who those key followers were and he intended that they be killed. Every war must have money and Jamie intended to find out who provided that money. Every war has goals and those who put those goals into plans. Jamie intended to find out who these people were and he intended to kill them. Every war needs money . To use a popular expression "No Bucks- No Buck Rogers". Jamie intended to find out how and who was financing this war. He intended to kill those who were financing this war and to steal their money.

During the time that Jamie and his men worked to learn Saudi culture a new group was created. It was founded and funded by Saudis and had a different approach than did the followers of Al Qaeda. This new group had seized portions of Syria and Iraq and established what they called a "Caliphate". Their goal was the same as that of Al Qaeda. To rule the world. They gave the Caliphate the name of Islamic State of Syria and the Levant or   ISIL.

Jamie gave his team specific tasks. Each member was to concentrate on various elements of the House of bin Laden, the House of Saud and ISIL. They were to write software and middleware programs to help Jamie analyze the massive data available to Jamie from the data bases of these three groups After a year in Saudi Arabia they were to return to their companies. John Devore was to look at ways that drones or other robotic devises could be used as weapons to kill. Dave Mandrake was to look at ways that his satellite could intercept radio signals and ways that it could send signals to the drones developed by John Devore. George Thornton was to develop the software and middleware programs needed by the computers which would guide the drones developed by John Devore. Bill Morgan would oversee the aeronautical challenges presented by John, Dave and George. Weldon Roberts, with his Nano Technology company was to look for ways to miniaturize all of the things which were to be used by the group. In particular Weldon was to look for lethal means of killing which could be miniaturized.

Jamie was to take this massive information, review it and decide what it meant.

By this time Jamie had become as Saudi as it was possible for him to be. He spoke Arabic with the accent common of a Saudi resident of Jeddah. He went to Mosque several times a week and was accepted, without notice, by the other worshipers. He remained low key and did what he could to avoid drawing attention to himself. When asked he described himself as a scholar.

Although his research was centered upon Saudi Arabia he had also visited Egypt, the Sudan, Jordan, Lebanon, Syria and Iran. He had easily obtained a Saudi name, a Saudi passport and a Saudi identity. By this time Jamie was convinced that Osama bin Laden was not the leader who had conceived and ordered the September 11, 2001 attack and the attacks which followed. Bin Laden was merely a "straw man" designed to distract attention from the real leader. Two shadowy organizations attracted the attention of Jamie. One of these organizations surprised Jamie. It was the worldwide organization known as the Masons. Jamie's father had been a member of this secretive organization. Over the centuries, since its' Creation, Masons had been condemned by Moslems, Jews and Christians. The Masonic Lodge, of which Jamie's father had been a member, was a benign organization which, despite its' secrets, sparked little controversy and did many good deeds. However, in his research Jamie found a link between Masonic lodges in the Arab world and a secretive order known as the Muslim Brotherhood. The Muslim Brotherhood had become very powerful in Egypt and, in the first democratic election in Egyptian history, had elected its leader as President. After a short time in office a military coup overthrew the newly elected President and he had been replaced by a brutal dictator. The Muslim Brotherhood was outlawed in Egypt and its President condemned to death.

Chapter Four-Urbana, Illinois and the "Burning Barn"

As a young man Jamie's face was almost handsome but not enough so that he could have served as a model for a cigarette ad or as a leading man in a Hollywood movie. He looked more like the leading man's best friend. His nose was well shaped and placed at about the proper place on his face. His reddish blond hair was curly and abundantly covered the top and sides of his head. He was a large man with a large frame spread over a body which stood more than six foot one tall. His pale complexion turned easily to red if he made the mistake of staying too long in sunlight.. He was a good athlete and in high school had won letters in football, basketball, cross country track and baseball. He had also been on his schools' Golden Gloves boxing team boxing in the 155 pound class. He had played college football and had been on his colleges Golden Glove boxing team boxing at 195 pounds. His blue eyes were at least as blue and as intense as those of the singer known as "Old Blue Eyes". Although he lacked the regional accent of the Midwestern United States he was indeed a "Midwesterner".

As a young boy he had fit in well in his Illinois hometown. He could have been used as a model of the sort of idyllic life for which the Mid-West is famous. He could have been the centerpiece of a Norman Rockwell painting. He had been a little Leaguer, a Sunday school pupil at the local Methodist Church, a newspaper boy delivering newspapers in the area around his neighborhood. He was born in a large Catholic hospital near a medium sized town in North Central Illinois. His parents had grown up on farms on opposite sides of Champaign County, Illinois. Champaign County is a very fertile county which annually produces large crops of soybeans and corn. It also serves as the home of the University of Illinois which is divided between the "twin cities" of Urbana and Champaign. Urbana was founded many years before Champaign. It had been founded by westward bound settlers who by the time they reached the area had gone as far West as they wanted to go. The two towns are divided by a single street and by their histories. In its' early days Urbana was a community of merchants who served the prosperous farmers of the area. It also served as a way station for settlers coming through the area on the way further west. The town prospered from its' central location and from the farmers who farmed the rich prairieland around the town. During the last part of the nineteenth century a railroad company decided to build a railroad south from Chicago to New Orleans which would take the railroad directly through the town of Urbana. Most small towns would have welcomed a railroad. Property values would soar and much additional commerce would have been created. That was not true of Urbana. It had become a genteel, prosperous town of merchants and tradesmen with large churches and good schools. It already had the land grant college which was to become the state University of Illinois. It was a well laid out town with a town center and straight, checkerboard streets. The town was horrified at the thought of having a noisy railroad through the center of town with noisy trains and rowdy railroad workers. The desire of the town for peace and tranquility was stronger than its desire for new commerce. So Urbana told the railroad it couldn't come through Urbana. Accordingly, the railroad company built its' tracks a few miles west of Urbana and named that stop on the railroad Champaign after the name of the County. Quickly a new town grew up around the depot and in a few years the Eastern edge of this town had reached the Western city limits of Urbana. Champaign is a word which is defined by *Webster's as a "wide, level open space".* Except for the twin cities of Urbana-Champaign, the area is wide, level open space. Over the years Champaign outgrew Urbana but the county seat of Champaign County remains in Urbana.

Jamie grew up in genteel Urbana. As he had grown out of the toddler stage his father had taken a position at the University in the Department of Agriculture. Jamie's parents had both grown up on farms in Champaign County. They had met at a Methodist Church picnic which had brought together Methodists from all over the area. Jamie was their first born and their only son. He was the older brother to two younger sisters. He went with his parents to Sunday School and Church at the First Methodist Church of Urbana every Sunday. His father taught one of the Sunday school classes. Methodist's emphasis free grace and individual responsibility based upon the theology first set out in the writings of John and Charles Wesley. It is not an extreme version of Christianity. As a Protestant church it fosters moderation but doesn't demand it. Jamie's parents practiced moderation. His father neither drank or smoked and during his lifetime Jamie never heard him use a profane word. His mother did like a sip of Mogen

David on certain occasions. Jamie might never have acquired a full vocabulary had it not been for his maternal grandfather, J.R. J.R. was a formidable man who smoked a pipe, chewed tobacco, had a shot of whiskey with breakfast and exposed Jamie to a complete vocabulary of obscene or profane expressions. J.R. had been born in East Tennessee in 1889 and had left school at age eight to work in a coal mine. By the age of 19 he was working as a Barber and helping to work the family farm with his 12 brothers and sisters. When he was 21 J.R. met Maude, Jamie's maternal grandmother, on the Cherokee Indian Reservation which covers large portions of the Smokey Mountains of Eastern Tennessee / Western North Carolina. J.R. was 27 when Jamie's mother was born. J.R. had worked at various jobs while trying to make a living from the poor soil of the East Tennessee Mountains. Among other things he had taken casks of moonshine whiskey on mules through the mountains to the Eastern seaboard. Like many others in East Tennessee J.R. had heard about the fertile farm lands of Illinois and when Jamie's mother was a year old J.R. had moved the family to Central Illinois. During the 1920's and 1930's J.R. prospered as a farmer and bought a 160 acres of his own. With only a second grade education he had found it necessary to teach himself math to avoid being cheated when he bought seed and other farm supplies from the merchants of the area. J.R. was also a very good mechanic and in 1934 he invented and patented a plough cleaner which would keep a plough clean as it was being pulled by a tractor. This made it possible for a farmer to till a field without numerous stops to clean the rich Illinois clay from the plough. J.R. couldn't get a farm implement manufacturer to make his plough cleaner so for two years

J.R. went to Gary, Indiana, loaded up his truck with steel and made the plough cleaners in his barn. They sold as fast as J.R. could make them and after two years J.R. sold the design to John Deere and became a rich man. Instead of retiring he bought more farm land. By the time Jamie was born J.R. was one of the richest farmers in Illinois. As Jamie grew up he would spend one month of each summer on the farm with J.R. and Maude. He would help tend their garden, feed the chickens, milk the cow, pull weeds from the rows of corn and soybeans and help with the many other tasks of a farm. Every Saturday morning during his stays on J.R's farm, J.R. would take Maude on the 16 mile drive east to Champaign. Saturday was the only day that Maude and J.R. would dress up. J.R. would rise early and take a shower in the shower he had built in the basement. The water came from a well and was pulled up from the depths by a

45

Windmill. After showering and shaving they would have a big breakfast of eggs, ham, biscuits, strawberry jam from Maude's garden, molasses and gravy, and big glasses of milk. J.R. would also have a shot of whiskey. After breakfast J.R. would put on his tailor made, cream colored suit and his well polished brown and white leather shoes and Maude would put on her favorite dress, which J.R. had bought for her from Marshall Fields in Chicago, and they would all go to town. J.R. would drive them to town in his Chrysler. He bought a new top of the line Chrysler every fall after the crop was sold. When television came to Champaign County J.R. was the first farmer to put up an antenna and buy a TV. When color TV was introduced J.R. was the first farmer in the county to buy a color TV. The first time Jamie ever saw color TV was a telecast of the Rose Bowl football game during a holiday gathering of the family.

J.R. taught Jamie to drive a tractor at the age of nine as soon as his legs were long enough to reach the pedals. When Jamie turned 12, JR let him drive the Chrysler to Champaign on the Saturday morning trips. Jamie was an excellent driver. He was tall for his age and well able to see over the big steering wheel of the Chrysler. One of the more memorable events Jamie experienced during the last summer he spent with J.R. and Maude was the tearing down of one of J.R's old barns so that he could replace it with a modern barn with an automated grain storage conveyor system. All old barns, over the years, would become the home for hundreds of rats and mice and as the old barn was to be torn apart the rodents would flee. J.R. had called in farmers from all over the area to surround the barn as it was torn apart and burned. The farmers, their children and their dogs surrounded the burning barn with clubs and as the barn was torn apart they beat to death hundreds of fleeing rodents. It was a sight Jamie would remember all of his life. People with clubs and dogs running in every direction. J.R. had surrounded the entire area with a sheet metal fence to keep any of the rodents from escaping. The bodies of the rats and mice formed a pile which was more than knee high and their bodies were shoveled back on to the burning barn. The barn burned for a day and a night until nothing was left but ashes.

Chapter 5-Free Masonry and the Muslim Brotherhood

The **Muslim Brotherhood** was founded in Ismailia, Egypt by Hassan al-Banna in March 1928 as an Islamist religious, political, and social movement.[1][2] The group spread to other Muslim countries but has its largest, or one of its largest, organizations in Egypt, where for many years it has been the largest, best-organized, and most disciplined political opposition force, despite a succession of government crackdowns in 1948, 1954, 1965 after plots, or alleged plots, of assassination and overthrow were uncovered. Following the 2011 Revolution the group was legalized, and in April 2011 it launched a civic political party called the Freedom and Justice Party (Egypt) to contest elections, including the 2012 presidential election when its candidate Mohamed Morsi became Egypt's first democratically elected President. One year later, however, following massive demonstrations, Morsi was overthrown by the military and arrested. In 2014, the organization had been declared a terrorist group and once again was suffering a severe crackdown. Morsi was executed by the Egyptian government.

The Muslim Brotherhood, in some respects, was organized like the Masons.

In the early 20th century the British had used Islam to help prop up support for the rulers it had installed in Jordan, Iraq, Saudi Arabia and Palestine after taking over the Middle East after World War I. Consequently most of the independence movements in those countries were led by men who wanted to put in place independent, secular governments. Men like Abdul Nasser in Egypt. To counter the rise of men like Nasser, the British promoted a resurgence in Islamic fundamentalism. During the period between World War I and II, the British had financed the beginnings of today's Islamic militancy.

Freemasonry appeared in Egypt after Napoleon's conquest of Egypt in 1798. The French established many Masonic lodges and most important Egyptian leaders were Masons. By 1957 there were more than 70 Masonic lodges in Egypt and leaders of the Nationalist and Wafd parties in Egypt were Masons. Two very important Islamic leaders in Egypt were also Masons. These Islamic leaders maintained close contacts with Masons in Britain. In 1899 the British governor of Egypt, Lord Cromer, made Shikh Mohammed Abduh the Grand Mufti of Egypt. This made him the "Pope of Islam". At the same time he was also the Masonic Grand Master of the United Lodge of Egypt.

Masonry has its' roots in medieval Britain and its' founding members were skilled craftsmen in the Masonry trades thus giving this secret society its' name. They had helped built many of the cathedrals which graced Britain and the organization they had given their name was initially meant to protect them from exploitation.

In 1930 a group of Masons, with funds provided by the Suez Canal Company, founded the Muslim Brotherhood in Egypt and built the brotherhoods first Mosque. In the next decade, with the support of the British government, the Muslim Brotherhood grew to more than 500,000 members. Like Masonry the Muslim Brotherhood was initially established as a charity. Unlike Masonry it was open only to Moslems. Like Masonry it was a secret society. Some described it as Masonry for Moslems. Like Masonry it was devoted to secrecy and was run according to a pyramidal command structure. The foot soldiers at the bottom often had no idea of the true goals of the leaders at the top.

Jamie's research convinced him that the leader at the tip of the pyramidal command structure of the modern Muslim Brotherhood was the person who had ordered the attacks against the US. Now he needed to find out who that person was and who else made up their pyramidal command structure. Furthermore, he was convinced that the real goal of the leaders was not to establish Moslem dominion over the world but to gain power for their version of a world government. Like in so many past eras Jamie believed that religion was being used to achieve power. The question, of course, was who was seeking power. Jamie, learned, much to his surprise that the person at the top of the pyramid was not a Moslem. This person was a hidden Hitler, trying to use Islam, to rule the world. Jamie was going to track down this Hitler and kill him.

By this time, Jamie knew more about the House of Saud than probably any person in the world. He knew who all of the leaders were and he knew everything it was possible to learn about them. They were for the most part, supporters of the Moslem Brotherhood and were promoters of the Wahhabi sect of Islam. The House of Saud were somewhere in the pyramid but great secrecy surrounded their activities.

By this time Jamie had sent all of his fellow researcher's home, to their respective areas, except for Bill Morgan who remained in Riyadh. Before the other four men had left Saudi Jamie had given each of them further tasks. They were to each provide Jamie with extensive reports on what they had concluded during their times in Saudi Arabia. He also asked them to be thinking of ways the group could achieve its goals. How they could kill the person at the tip of the pyramid. How they could kill the key members of the pyramidal command structure. How they could deprive the organization of the money used to wage this war. How they could destroy the capacity of the Saudi to gain wealth and influence from oil.

The founder of the Muslim Brotherhood, Hasan al-Banna once said of the plans of the Muslim

Brotherhood " *We need three generations for our plans, one to listen, one to fight, and one to win*".

It was in July that Jamie found the man who was at the head of the pyramid. He had done so by diligent and careful review of all the information he and his friends had accumulated. His discovery proved once again that things are not always what they seem.

The Arab world has always been filled with secrecy, intrigue and duplicity. Much of this they have gotten from the British.

Chapter Six –Grandmother's Log Cabin

Jamie's paternal grandparents lived on the other side of Champaign County, East of Urbana, with the poorest farm land in Champaign County. Their farm was in the only part of Champaign County which was not flat as a checkerboard. Their farm was hilly and a small river ran through it. His paternal grandparents, although Methodists like his maternal grandparents, were much different. Their ancestors had come to America in 1607 to flee persecution in England. These ancestors had been Huguenots and their strict religion had made them enemies everywhere they lived. By the time Jamie's paternal grandfather had been born the family had become Methodists. This grandfather and grandmother had lived in Champaign County all of their lives and their parents were some of the original settlers back when Illinois was still the "wild" West. They lived in a house which had been built around a log cabin which had been built by his paternal grandmother's father. Jamie's paternal grandfather had died when Jamie was eight. For one month each summer he went to stay on the farm with, Bertha, his paternal grandmother. She was a formidable woman. Jamie's father had been born during Bertha's second marriage. Her first husband had been killed in Cuba as he followed Teddy Roosevelt up San Juan Hill. Bertha's father had been born in Ireland and in addition to the farm was a country doctor with a medical degree from Harvard Medical School. The House sat on a hill two hundred yards above a slow flowing river. The porch had a swinging bench from which Jamie could swing and watch the cranes and ducks swoop down to the river. The River was one of Jamie's favorite places. When his father was growing up on the farm he made spending money trapping beavers and minks so he could sell their fur to fur companies. The river contained some huge fish- Carp and Buffalo- which often grew to weigh more than 100 pounds. Jamie enjoyed sitting on the banks of the river and watching tadpoles and fish swim by. He also learned to swim in the river when he fell in one afternoon when no one was around to save him. The farm was a poor one which had barely given Bertha enough income to support Jamie's father, his brother and three sisters. But the family was hardworking and always managed to get by without government handouts. Unlike the farmhouse of JR and Maude, his father's home place lacked indoor plumbing. During cold weather the house was heated by a large coal burning furnace in the living room. The house was one of the last in Champaign County to get electricity. Despite the lack of modern conveniences Jamie's loved staying with Bertha for one month each summer. Bertha was a Philosopher and a Poet. She had a library full of old books which Jamie couldn't find in the modern library in Urbana. An old barn contained a buckboard which had been pulled by horses during the time his father lived on the farm. The barn also contained farm implements from the days before farming became mechanized. It almost always had new litters of kittens. If Jamie could find the kittens early on he could tame them as they grew up. If he found them too late they became wild and would disappear into the woods to be eaten by foxes or raccoons.

Urbana was a good place for Jamie to grow up. It is a town of many tall trees, parks, and neat quiet streets and sidewalks. The prosperity of the town is evident by its' many fine homes of brick and stone with spacious rooms and well tended yards. When Jamie was 9 his father bought a vacate lot in a quiet neighborhood across from a small park. It was the last vacant lot in a neighborhood containing many fine old homes owned by Professors and other employees of the University. Just after his father had bought the lot dirt had been scooped out for the basement. Jamie was sitting on a big mound of dirt watching the concrete for the basement as it was being poured. A boy Jamie's age came by and Jamie playfully threw a small clod of dirt at the other boy. The other boy's name was George and he lived a few houses away. Jamie and George immediately became close friends and would remain so until George, who grew up to become a CPA, died of cancer of the lymph nodes at the age of 33.

The residents of the house next door to Jamie's house were Polish immigrants who had fled Poland after the First World War. Professor Molinski was 73 years old when Jamie moved in next door. The Professor and his wife were childless and a bond between them and Jamie was immediately formed. Most evenings the Professor, who had taught Electrical Engineering at the University for 20 years, enjoyed sitting on his front porch to smoke a pipe full of fragrant tobacco, drink iced coffee brought out to him by his wife, Sofia, and talking to Jamie. Jamie never tired of listening to the Professor's stories. The professor was a genius and quickly discovered that Jamie was too. Years before the Professor had invented a process which enabled a movie maker to put sound on film and he taught Jamie everything he knew about electricity and electrical systems. He taught Jamie how to take radios, televisions and other electrical devices apart and how they worked. The Professor was a prolific inventor with a basement lab in which he gave Jamie a college level education in electrical engineering before Jamie was old enough for high school. The professor also had a deep interest in computer technology and helped give Jamie an early look at the computer science which would capture Jamie's attention all of his life.

Across from Jamie's house was a small park in the middle of which was a statute of Abraham Lincoln holding a law book. The inscription at the foot of the statute said "A. Lincoln, Lawyer"

Urbana and the University offered much to Jamie and he often spent days with his friend George visiting the Natural History Museum or the farms operated by the schools Department of Agriculture. They particularly liked the Museum of Natural History which contained dinosaur skeletons, Indian artifacts and stuffed animals. They also liked the University Observatory where they could look through powerful telescopes into space. Jamie was always a welcome guest in the Department of Electrical Engineering where the Professor liked to show him what he was teaching to his students. It delighted the Professor to introduce his students to a twelve year old boy who knew more than they did.

From age 10 Jamie had a newspaper route delivering newspaper to homes around the park. At certain times of the year he also sold small pear shaped tomatoes and other produce which had been declared excess by Maude from her garden. Jamie packed this produce in old Quaker Oat boxes and delivered it to favored customers who would always ask Jamie to remember them the next time he had something available.

Jamie's bucolic life in Champaign County ended when he was 13. President Eisenhower, keeping a campaign promise, had ended the war in Korea and the United States suffered a short recession. The recession lasted just long enough to ruin his father. In addition to being a Professor at the University his father had developed a housing subdivision on the outskirts of Urbana. His father found himself with 60 unsold homes when no one was buying. The family home would have to be sold to pay the debts that the housing subdivision had created. After paying all of his debts, Jamie's father, unable to face the embarrassment of failure, quit his job at the University, bought a 30 foot house trailer, hooked it up to the family car, packed the family and their possessions in it and headed south towards Florida.

Chapter Seven- The investigation

Before Jamie and his team could begin looking for those responsible for the attacks against the US, they needed to learn how to speak, read and write Arabic. By the end of the year Jamie and his team had mastered Arabic and were living in Saudi Arabia. Jamie, using the best search engines, had read thousands of pages of information, in English on the Internet regarding the attacks. He also had researchers working for him in one of his companies in Ireland which reviewed French, Arabic, German, Italian, Urdu, Sikh, Farsi and Russian web sites looking for information which would be translated into English and sent to Jamie. Much of what Jamie read was written on behalf of governments or organizations who simply wanted to confuse readers. Endless, absurd conspiracy theories implicating space aliens, dead Nazis, etc. Jamie sifted through what he read and anything which seemed plausible went into his data bank. After he could read Arabic he developed a search engine which could sift through Arabic data using certain key words. Jamie also had complete access to all the data bases used by members of the House of Saud, the House of bin Laden and a number of sub groups of the Muslim Brotherhood including ISIL. His company had helped set up security firewalls for the House of Saud, for the House of bin Laden and ISIL so it was easy for him to bypass these firewalls and read all of the private correspondence of these groups. However, Jamie knew that many of the decisions made by members of the House of Saud were made in private meetings which were not recorded and which did not end up in computer data banks. He also knew that when important decisions were put in writing the House of Saud would use elaborate codes. Jamie had access to some of the best code breaking software to ever come into existence and he could penetrate the most complex code easily. Jamie believed that following the money which had been used to finance the attacks was the first step in learning who was responsible for the attacks. It was evident that most of the money came from the House of Saud but the finances of the House of Saud were extremely complex. Jamie's own finances were very complex but were simple in comparison to those of the House of Saud. Tracing money was very difficult since many countries permit bank accounts not linked to a particular person. Even in countries like the United States and Great Britain, it was possible to have bank accounts which did not disclose the principals who controlled them. Many bank accounts were in the names of dummy companies or employed layers of fictitious names. One common thread always existed in any bank account regardless of how well hidden the principal. The bank needed to have payment instructions and documentation which would empower the bank to release funds. In some cases all that was necessary to release funds from a bank account was a secret code. Rarely did funds go directly from a bank to anyone involved with the attacks. More often ordinary credit cards or atm cards issued to dummy companies were the mechanism which permitted payments to the "soldiers" who carried out attacks. Identifying the principals in a dummy company was very difficult since many of these principals used fictitious names. It was easier to trace the source of money coming into accounts than it was to determine who had authorized money going out. In the early days of his investigation Jamie determined that most of the money going into bank accounts used to finance the attacks came from the House of Saud. Often the money was sent through Islamic charities or Islamic religious organizations. The key was to determine who in the House of Saud authorized the release of monies sent to finance the attacks. The House of Saud was organized very much like the Italian Mafia or the Japanese Yakuza. It was also ruled much like the Masons with one person, the King, at the top of the pyramid and various Princes spread throughout the pyramid.

The House of Saud consists of at least six distinct branches all of whom trace their ancestry back to an 18th Century founder, Muhammad bin Saud. The "Royal" section, with the descendants of this 18th Century founder, produced the modern founder of Saudi Arabia, Abd al-Aziz,

King Ibn Saud. A separate branch of the family, known as the "Cadet" section has produced many who can call themselves "His Highness" or "Prince". Many of these "Princes" exercise immense power within the family but under the constitution enacted by King Ibn Saud in 1932 only his sons could become King. King Ibn Saud is said to have had more than 235 wives during his reign which ended with his death in 1952. From these wives it is said that King Ibn-Saud had at least 43 sons and more than 50 daughters. The allegiance of the King's sons revolves around which mother and from which tribe they came. This could influence how they were brought up, how they were educated, marriage choices and relationship to the House of al-Sheikh. The House of al –Sheikh was the lineage coming from the founder of the Wahhabi sect of Islam, Muhammad ibn Abd ai-Wahhabi. King Ibn-Saud many marriages often served to enlarge his kingdom by creating alliances with tribes and rivals. Only those who descend through the Royal Section, descendants of Abd al-Aziz, could become King. By this time the King of Saudi Arabia was King Salman who was in his eighties. By the middle of the year Jamie had a very good idea of who were the members of the pyramid from top on down. In 2006 The King of Saudi Arabia, King Fahd, who had been completely disabled, mentally and physically, from a stroke he had suffered, years before, died. King Fahd belonged to the Sudayri faction from the Al-Sudayri tribe. The new King, Abdullah, had been serving as de facto leader since King Fahd had suffered a severe stroke in 1995. King Abdullah came from the Al-Shammar tribe, a powerful tribe from Northern Arabia. During his years as Crown Prince he had managed to make the Al-Shammar tribe the most powerful and important segment of the House of Saud. When King

Abdullah died Jamie was watching with keen interest the struggle for power within the House of Saud. The new King was the former foreign minister Saud al-Faysal. King Faysal was the son of the former and greatly respected first King Faysal. To some extent the ascension of King Abdullah followed by King Faysal made it clear that the descendants of Abd ai Wahhab would set the direction of the House of Saud.

Some of the sons of King Ibd- Saud had died and some had no interest in seeking power in the House of Saud. Five of these sons now lived outside the Kingdom in opulence in Europe and had very little power within the House of Saud. They had received large sums of money upon the death of King Ibn Saud and still received large sums of money from the House of Saud. Nine other of his sons had withdrawn from the struggle for power and lived in quiet luxury in Saudi Arabia. Because of the Saudi

71

adherence with Wahhabism no female members of the House of Saud had direct power in the decisions of the House of Saud. However, some of the Princes were greatly influenced by their mothers or wives and, in some cases by sisters or daughters.

By now Jamie appeared to be a Saudi and he was accepted as being a Moslem at the Mosque he attended. However, he maintained a very low profile. Unlike Saudis he did not have a staff of servants to serve him. Mustafa was his only employee and Mustafa's wife did all the shopping. Mustafa and his wife lived in the same modest complex as Jamie. Jamie had built a secret office under his home in which he spent most of his time. He often went with Mustafa to socialize with Bedouin elders in Saudi Arabia and Yemen. They would sit for hours and discuss the great events of the day and sip tea and eat Bedouin food.

They would gossip about the doings of the House of Saud.

The House of Saud was funded by the billions of dollars which came into the bank accounts of the House of Saud through the vast oil production of Saudi Arabia. This money was distributed throughout the House of Saud based upon distribution determined by what the House of Saud called the counsel of 50. A portion of the oil revenues was distributed among non members of the House of Saud. Many members of the House of Saud supplemented their income shares by collecting protection money from Saudi businesses. No Saudi business regardless of how large or small escaped from paying tribute to members of the House of Saud. The House of Saud assigned territories to its members who could prey on any business in their territory.

Jamie's feelings towards the House of Saudi and towards Saudis in general was hostile. Most members of the House of Saud were lazy, spoiled, greedy and corrupt. Most followed the tenets of Islam only in public. Many of them exploited everyone around them. They exploited other family members and other Saudi, particularly women but most of all they exploited the guest workers who had come to Saudi Arabia from many countries to do the jobs Saudis refused to do. Any attractive woman or man working as a guest worker in a Saudi household could expect to be required to provide sexual services to the men in the household. In many households guest workers were held in what amounted to slavery. In the 21st century slavery was still common in Saudi Arabia. Members of the House of Saud often violated the Islamic law which formed the basis for Saudi law but rarely were they punished.

Jamie's investigation was taking a great deal of time and energy. In the latter part of the year he had succeeded in selling all of the companies that he owned. To limit the income taxes he would need to pay all of the proceeds from the sales of his various companies were funneled into a new company he had formed. The new company was based in Switzerland and had 200 employees Its' employees performed tasks which helped Jamie and his five friends answer the question Jamie had asked himself at the beginning who had murdered his family? The new company also possessed some very interesting weapons which Jamie intended to use once he knew who to use them against. His new company was run by his five friends and held assets with a value of 80 billion dollars. The new company was based in Switzerland. Jamie had renounced his U.S. citizenship earlier and had become a citizen of Switzerland. He had also obtained Saudi citizenship.

During his investigation additional attacks occurred against the United States. The President and Vice President of the United States were assassinated. In addition a massive attack on the Oil, Gas and Electrical infrastructure of the United States had taken place. Saboteurs destroyed key portions of the electrical grid system in the U.S. This plunged the nation into a crisis unlike any it had seen before. There was a nationwide breakdown in law enforcement. Farmers lacked the fuel to plant or to harvest crops. Food could not be moved from area to area. Food that would normally reach US markets from other countries couldn't get through. Schools, universities, hospitals closed. Enforcement of the US borders ceased. However, few Mexicans or Canadians wanted to come to a country with limited electricity or few fuel supplies. To the contrary large numbers of Americans were fleeing to Mexico and Canada. The government was forced to declare martial law and every state called out their National Guards to help distribute food and water. Riots took place in every major city as hungry and thirsty people sought food or water.

In Saudi Arabia Jamie worried that he might not live long enough to complete his mission and gain his revenge. He was now 71 years of age and it appeared to him that the world was starting to fall apart. The disastrous situation in the United States was causing ripples all over the world and, in particular, in Saudi Arabia. So many countries depended upon the United States for income. The Saudis could sell their oil elsewhere but without the U.S. as a consuming nation the Saudis could not get as good a price. If the U.S. could prevent additional attacks they could repair their oil pipelines and refineries in a few months if they could restore electrical power.

However, to restore electrical power they needed fuel. The disastrous situation threw the world into a major depression . Countries which had depended upon the US for business or for economic aid suffered greatly. Finally Jamie completed the puzzle concerning the pyramid of the organization which was planning and carrying out the attacks on the U.S. The attacks which had killed his family and which had plunged the US into a depression which was worse than any that the country had ever experienced. Now it was time for him to act. It was the time which his Rage had earned him. It was the time which would reward him for all of the work that he had done.

Chapter Eight-Graceland Subdivision

When Jamie's father left Urbana to move to Florida Jamie was very sad to leave his friends in Urbana behind. He also knew he would miss being close to his grandparents. At the same time the move really seemed like an adventure to Jamie. He and his two younger sisters were also excited about living in the house trailer. It was a bit like camping out. His father expected they would make it to Florida in five days and Jamie enjoyed seeing new sites along the way. The first day of their trip was exciting. It took Jamie's father a few miles to adjust to pulling the 30 foot house trailer and several times the house trailer nearly jackknifed and came close to pulling the Chrysler off of the road. After the first day Jamie's father let him do all the driving. All of the driving was on two lane highways and Jamie was a better driver. He was already taller than his father and quickly adapted to pulling the trailer. By the end of the second day the family had reached Memphis, Tennessee and pulled into a nice trailer park to spend the evening. Their car was not air conditioned and it had been a hot, muggy day. The weather in

Memphis was more than a 100 degrees and Jamie's

father decided they would rest for a day in Memphis

before heading on to Florida. Jamie unhooked the

trailer and the family went for a drive around Memphis.

It was a nice clean city with many nice parks. The

family particularly liked the Memphis Zoo which was

located in a large park in the center of the city. The park

had many large trees which made it cooler than other

areas of the city. Jamie's father heard on the radio that

the temperature was 110 degrees in Florida. Jamie's

mother, Jamie and his two sisters liked Memphis and

wanted to stay a couple of more days. The next day

Jamie's father gave him $5.00 so Jamie could catch a

bus to downtown Memphis to see the city a bit more. In

the meantime Jamie's father decided to look for

employment in Memphis. Jamie stood at the bus stop

in front of the trailer park and when the bus pulled up

Jamie got on, paid the

fare and walked to the back of the empty bus and sat down. The bus didn't move. In a few moments the bus driver walked to the back of the bus and told Jamie " Son you can't sit here in the back" and pointed to a sign which said "colored passengers rear seats only". "What color are you" the bus driver asked Jamie. Jamie had to stop and think and replied "Mostly White". "What do you mean mostly? The bus driver asked. " I'm one fourth Cherokee" replied Jamie proudly. The bus driver said "You look white to me" and waived Jamie to the front of the bus. "Where you from son?" asked the bus driver. Jamie replied "Illinois, but my mother was born in Tennessee." The bus driver explained to Jamie that in Memphis when a boy talked to his elders he was to say "Yes Sir or Yes Ma'am". Jamie quickly said "Yes Sir" and took a seat. The bus driver chuckled quietly to himself as the bus pulled away from the curb. This tall young boy, nearly six foot tall and weighing 115 pounds soaking wet wasn't sure that he was white. With his red hair and pale skin he didn't look like an Indian and he certainly didn't look "colored". The bus moved slowly towards downtown Memphis and by the time it got downtown it was full with most of the other passengers being "colored". Memphis had recently won an award as the cleanest city in the United States and it did look good. But Memphis was a very strange place to Jamie. Downtown Memphis is located on a river bluff overlooking the Mississippi River. The city stretches from West to East which means that the Arkansas bank of the river is closer to downtown than most Memphis neighborhoods. It was a bright, hot sunny day and Jamie walked from one end of downtown Memphis to the other. He quickly discovered that Memphis had two separate downtowns. The southern end of Main street crossed the "colored" section of Memphis at

Beale Street. He understood that Memphians of African ancestry were called "colored". Back in Urbana he had thought very little about race. One of his best friends on the basketball team was a young black kid from one of the few black families in Urbana. Jamie walked down Beale Street which looked very exotic to Jamie. Most of the people on Beale Street were "Colored" and the street was lined with pawn shops, cheap clothing stores, taverns and pool halls. He could sense that most of the people were wondering what he was doing on Beale Street. He came across a small park which had a statute of W.C. Handy which said that he was the father of the "Blues". That day Jamie learned more about segregation. Back in Urbana the only segregation was by sex. Here in Memphis there were separate drinking fountains, separate entrances to businesses and some businesses which would only accept whites. The downtown Woolworth lunch counter had a large sign which said "Whites' Only." When Jamie got to the movie theatre on Main Street he tried to buy a ticket to see the movie and asked to sit in the balcony where he had always sat back in Urbana. The ticket teller told him that the balcony was reserved for "Colored". This seemed really silly to Jamie. Weren't they all going to see the same movie. Did the water at the "colored" drinking fountain taste different. Despite the silliness of segregation Jamie liked Memphis. When he got back to the trailer park that evening he found that his father had found a job in Memphis at a local University and that the family was not going any further south. The next day his father sold the house trailer and moved the family into a nice house near the Memphis Zoo.

The new house was in a nice neighborhood about a block from a set of railroad tracks. On the other side of the tracks was a small park with an asphalt basketball court. A few days after the family moved into their new home Jamie walked across the tracks to the basketball court and began shooting baskets with his basketball. The court was empty when he first arrived. A couple of young black boys about Jamie's age showed up and stood at the edge of the Court and watched Jamie shoot. After a few minutes Jamie asked if they would like to get up a game. The boys hesitated for a few moments and talked among themselves before drifting on to the court to shoot baskets. They were very polite and called Jamie "Sir" which really confused him. Jamie introduced himself, as he had been taught to do, by offering a handshake. This really confused the other boys. No white person had ever offered to shake their hands. However, they knew this was a "colored" playground and so they asked Jamie "Where are you from?" Jamie told them he lived right down the street and had just moved to Memphis from Illinois. Upon hearing this the boys relaxed. That explained Jamie's strange conduct. They quickly got up a game of four on four. For the rest of the Summer Jamie played basketball with his new friends at the "colored" playground. By the time school started Jamie's basketball skills were well honed.

Things changed quickly when school started. Jamie was entering the eighth grade at a junior high which had 7th, 8th and 9th graders. It was, of course, an all white school. All of his basketball friends went off to a "colored" school not far away. Jamie felt like an outsider when school began. He didn't talk like the other kids. His accent was pure Illinois. The first day after school a ninth grader who was known as the school bully confronted Jamie on the edge of the school grounds and started insulting him and trying to pick a fight. Jamie didn't do anything until the boy tried to grab Jamie. The other boy was about Jamie's height but was 30 pounds heavier. Back in Illinois, one of Jamie's cousins, who had returned to Illinois after serving in the Army in Korea, had taught Jamie Judo so when the other boy tried to grab Jamie, Jamie grabbed his arm and flipped him high in the air. When the startled boy got to his feet Jamie flipped him again. After that first day word got around the school about Jamie and his Judo skills. The bully became Jamie's friend. Jamie also went out for the school's football team and although he didn't weigh much he was unusually strong for his size and he was tall and he made the team. Being on the football team helped him get accepted at the school despite his mid western accent. His closest friends in the school were Jewish. The school was not far from a large synagogue so many Jewish families lived in the area so they could walk to temple on

Sabbath. The Jewish kids seemed less inclined to berate Jamie for his "Yankee" accent and they recognized that Jamie was a very smart "kid". Quickly Jamie became part of the "Jewish" crowd at the school. Some of the other "goyem" at the school even thought Jamie was Jewish despite the fact that he didn't look like what they thought Jewish kids looked like. When the first school dance came around Jamie didn't plan to go. He didn't have a girl friend he could ask. A week before the dance one of his friends, Avron, asked Jamie if he had a "date" and when Jamie said "No" Avron arranged for Jamie to take Janel. Janel was a quiet, slender, dark haired girl who was in Jamie's home room class. For that dance and the other social affairs at the school for that year she became Jamie's date. She was cute and they got along well but Jamie's hormones were not yet controlling his life. He had recently seen a photo of Marilyn Monroe in a magazine being circulated by one of his friends and it had interested him but he wasn't sure why. His friends were beginning to talk about sex but had some misconceptions as to what was involved. Jamie's ideas about sex were pretty vague. He had heard from other boys that sex consisted of the male placing his penis in the anus of a female. Of course the boys didn't say penis or anus. They said "dick" and "ass". The thought didn't appeal to Jamie but he was beginning to notice girls quite a bit more as he finished the 8th grade and neared his 14th Summer. The last dance of the school year, with Janel, was more exciting than other dances had been. It had been held at the Jewish Community Center near his school. During the dance he and Janel had taken a break from the dance, wondered through the building and found a sofa in a quiet and dark room. They sat next to each other and Jamie decided to "cop a feel" which other boys had often talked about. Janel didn't have a whole lot for Jamie to feel but she also decided she wanted to cop a feel and so she put her hand on Jamie's penis which very quickly became erect. They both stopped right away and as they returned to the dance they both felt strangely happy without knowing why.

As summer approached Jamie reflected upon what had been for him a good year. He had made all city on the football team and all state on the basketball team. Many observers considered him to be the best, white, 8th grade basketball player in the state. They attributed this to the fact that Jamie had grown up in the Midwest where basketball was a religion.

After two years in Central Memphis, Jamie's father bought a house in a subdivision known as "Graceland" and moved the family to the suburbs. Whitehaven was a suburb of Memphis which stretched from the Southern city limits of Memphis to the Mississippi state line. Graceland was a new subdivision of nice brick homes in an area of rolling hills and pleasant houses with big well kept yards. At the front of the subdivision facing the highway was an old Southern mansion which was being used as a church.

Jamie was fifteen when the family moved to Graceland. Each Summer he would return to Urbana to work on J.R's farm. J.R. paid Jamie well and when Jamie returned to Memphis at the end of the Summer he had earned enough money to own his own car. He bought a blue Chevrolet convertible. He had returned to Memphis just a few days before school was scheduled to begin. He was scheduled to be a 10th grader. Jamie was in the front yard of the family home polishing his car under a big oak tree when he saw a young girl walking down the street. By this time Jamie had a better, more accurate view of what sex was all about but he had never gotten past the groping stage with the farm girls he had met while he was working in Illinois. His father had told him about the birds and the bees and had warned Jamie about the hazards of teen age pregnancy. He had told Jamie that if he got a girl pregnant he would have to get married and would not be able to go to college on a basketball scholarship. At that time going to college on a basketball scholarship was Jamie's goal in life. The feelings he got playing basketball were almost sexual in nature. He loved the feeling he got when a shot from the top of the circle got nothing but net.

As the young girl walked past where Jamie was standing he was totally mesmerized. He had never seen anything like this girl anywhere, anytime before. She was the most beautiful girl Jamie had ever seen. As Jamie learned later her name was Donna and she was only fourteen. She was wearing a pair of tight white shorts which did wonderful things to her waist and hips. She wore a white bare midriff halter top covering her breasts. Jamie was totally paralyzed by what he saw. She had a deep brown tan which contrasted sharply with what she was wearing. Jamie guessed her to be about 5-4 and 100 pounds. Her legs, hips, waist and torso were the shapeliest Jamie had ever seen. Her youthful breasts stretched her halter top. She had

a well tapered waist and slender feminine hips. Her brown

hair was tied in the back with a red ribbon and her neck and

beautiful face sent chills through Jamie. She had a small

delicate nose and a full sensuous mouth. She looked nothing

like the Illinois farm girls with which he had spent time that

summer. Jamie stood there with his mouth open. All sorts of

thoughts ran through his mind. To hell with playing college

basketball he thought. All of a sudden he was willing to take

his chances. Jamie watched as she turned into a driveway two

houses down the hill. He immediately rushed into the house

looking for his 14 year old sister, Helen. He demanded that

Helen go down the street and find out who this girl was and

report back to him. Helen thought it was pretty funny. She

had never seen her brother so frantic. Normally he was the

coolest kid around. Helen immediately went down the street

and introduced herself to Donna. She told Donna that her

brother would like to meet

her the next day when she took her daily walk. So it came to pass that Jamie met Donna. Every late afternoon Donna would take an evening walk which all the men and boys in the neighborhood anxiously awaited. The next day Helen walked with her and when they got to the front yard where Jamie was sitting on his car Helen introduced Donna to Jamie. It was one of the happiest days in Jamie's life and one he would remember until the day he died. Every evening after that until school started Jamie walked with Donna. He felt like he was ten foot tall when he was with her and he could hardly wait until they could be alone. Her brown eyes seemed to twinkle when Jamie looked into them and her soft Southern accent sounded like music to him. He didn't care what she was saying he just liked being with her. She never wore make up because her mother thought she was too young to do so. Her complexion could best be described as peaches and dark cream. Unfortunately for Jamie Donna wasn't allowed to date and her parents had told her she couldn't go on a date with a boy until she was 15. That was almost a year away. However, her parents didn't forbid Jamie from hanging around the house. When school started Donna rode to school each morning with Jamie. He remained after school each day for football practice so Donna would ride the school bus home each afternoon. This bothered Jamie because he was afraid she would sit next to another boy so he declared that he was going to quit the football team so he could drive Donna home each afternoon. His sister, Helen, who thought this whole thing with Jamie and Donna was pretty silly, solved the problem by telling Jamie not to worry she would sit next to Donna on the school bus ride home each afternoon. The year went by quickly for Jamie. Each day after football practice or basketball practice or track or baseball practice he would go home, have dinner and head to Dona's house. Some evenings they would sit in a swing on her front porch and watch the sun go down.

Other sunny evenings they would go into the garden in Dona's back yard and cultivate vegetables. Donna also liked to tend the flowers she had planned in the front yard. She particularly fussed about the orchids she was tending. She looked even more beautiful when she was in the middle of one of her flower beds. Donna was always the one who decided what to do. Whatever, she said was fine with Jamie. In the fall Donna had her 15th birthday and could finally go out on a date with Jamie. She had to be home by 11 p.m. and could only go out on Saturday nights. On Friday nights she and Jamie would go to the drive in movies with her parents. They got to sit in the backseat but her parents made them watch the movie and they couldn't sit as close to each other as Jamie wanted. The first date Jamie had with Donna was at a school dance. All the girls wore fluffy formal dresses with lots of petticoats. The boys wore sports coats. Jamie wore a white sports coat and Donna wore a pink formal with five petticoats. At the dance

Jamie was absolutely sure that Donna was the best looking girl at the dance and from the looks she got from other boys he wasn't the only one who thought so.

Donna was an only child and very close to her mother who had told her that she should "save herself" until she got married. Her mother had warned her about the passion of teenage boys and how to control it. After the dance Jamie had taken Donna to a bluff overlooking the Mississippi River which was a popular "Lover's Lane". Donna would let Jamie kiss her, as he had done many times before but she kept his hands tightly controlled so he couldn't squeeze her breasts or stroke her thighs. Jamie "behaved" himself because he didn't want to make Donna angry. He was also concerned about other boys asking her out. Her parents had forbid her to go "steady" with anyone and this bothered Jamie. Jamie was very popular at school because of his athletic ability. Good grades came easily to Jamie. He let it be known around school that he would be very unhappy if any of the other boys asked Donna out and, accordingly, none of them did. By now Jamie weighed 165 pounds and had begun to fill out his 6-1 frame. In addition to being a Judo master he was on his school's Golden Glove boxing team. When Donna was 16 several of her classmates persuaded her to enter a local beauty contest. Jamie didn't like the idea because he didn't want anyone to pay attention to Donna except him. Donna won the contest and her photo was in the local newspaper. A few days after her photo appeared she got a telephone call from someone who worked for the man who had bought the mansion at the front of their subdivision asking Donna if she would like to go out on a date with this man. Donna immediately said no because she knew her parents wouldn't let her go out with someone that much older. The man in the mansion was 23. She was asked if she would like to meet the man in the mansion and she said yes but she wanted to bring her boyfriend. A few days later Donna and Jamie drove up the circular driveway to the mansion. They were in Jamie's new Chevrolet to which he had applied 5 coats of black paint. The car had glass pipes and purred as they approached the front door. Several men were waiting for them at the front door. One of them had black hair and sideburns and was wearing a black leather jacket under which was a pink shirt with the collar turned up. The man's mouth gaped open as Donna was escorted from the car by Jamie. Donna was indeed the beauty he had seen in her photo. Jamie held out his hand and introduced himself and then he introduced Donna. The man slowly extended his hand and said in a voice familiar to millions "Hi "I'm Elvis Presley". Elvis introduced his friends and they stood around the front door talking. Elvis was smitten by Donna but during the conversation learned that they had an Uncle in common and that Donna was his cousin. He could also sense the bond between Jamie and Donna and the protective aura Jamie extended around her. Jamie was wearing his letterman jacket and he explained to Elvis what everything on the jacket meant. The miniature gold football and miniature gold basketball meant Jamie had lettered in those sports. The jacket also said All State and All County and Jamie explained that he had won these honors. Elvis was almost as impressed by Jamie as he was by Donna and he asked Jamie if he could bring some of his friends by the following Sunday to play touch football at the school behind Elvis's mansion. Jamie quickly agreed to do so. It was a very nice visit and the next Sunday Jamie and some of his friends from the high school came by and played a game of touch football against Elvis and his friends. Elvis tried hard but he wasn't really a very good athlete. Jamie thought he ran like a girl. During the game Elvis dislocated his thumb. The dislocation caused him to have to delay a movie he was scheduled to make so the studio re-wrote his contract forbidding him to play football again. Over the next year or so Elvis invited Jamie and

Donna to many of his parties. He would rent a roller skating rink or an amusement park or a movie theatre after they had closed and invite his friends to come have a party. There were always a lot of beautiful girls at Elvis's parties but all the men, including Elvis, agreed that Donna was always the best looking.

By 1959 Jamie and Donna had agreed that they would marry as soon as Donna graduated from high school which was two years away. Dona's parents had become concerned that Jamie was too much of a dominating influence on Donna. They liked Jamie but they wanted Donna to go out with other boys. They were puzzled that none of the boys at her high school would ask her out. It wasn't that other boys didn't want to ask her out but no one in the area who knew Jamie wanted to risk his wrath.

In 1959 Donna's mother took it upon herself to match Donna with the son of one of her friends who lived on the other side of Memphis more than 30 miles away so she arranged for this friend's son to take

Donna to a dance held by the Daughters of the Confederacy.

The boy's name was Dewey and he had never seen Donna

but obeyed his mother and agreed to take her to the dance.

On the night of the dance Dewey drove up Donna's

driveway, parked his car and went to the door. Donna's

mother let him in and seated him on a couch. When Donna

came out Dewey thought he had died and gone to heaven.

Donna was the most beautiful girl he had ever seen. Donna

didn't like the idea of going out with anyone but Jamie but

she had agreed to do so to please her parents. Dewey

escorted Donna to his car not knowing that Jamie was

watching them with field glasses from a window in his house.

Jamie followed them to the dance and sat in his car for three

hours waiting for the dance to end. It was driving him crazy

thinking of Donna inside dancing with Dewey. After the

dance Dewey wanted to take Donna out to a lover's lane but

she insisted that they go

straight home. When they got to her house Dewey walked her to the door and at the door tried to kiss her. Donna turned her face so his kiss grazed her cheek. She thanked Dewey and he floated away to his car certain that he would go out with Donna again. He would demand that his mother make it possible. Unbeknownst to Dewey Jamie had followed them from the dance to Donna's and after Dewey had left the house Jamie followed him down the road to an open area where he forced Dewey's car to the side of the Road. Dewey had no idea who Jamie was. All he knew was that a very angry young man had forced him off the road and dragged him from the car and appeared to be about to beat him badly. Fortunately for Dewey Donna's father had seen Jamie follow Dewey's car and he had followed them. He arrived just in time to drag Jamie off of Dewey. Jamie was yelling out to Dewey " Don't ever call Donna again. If you come over to this side of town again you'll need to get false teeth because I will knock out all your regular teeth." Dewey shook all the way back to his home on the other side of Memphis. He had never seen anyone so angry. He never asked his mother to set up a date with Donna again.

Donna's parents were furious at Jamie and they forbade Donna to go out with him again. Two months went by and Jamie was miserable. So was Donna. None of the other boys at school would ask her out and it didn't really make any difference. She only wanted to go out with Jamie. She had decided years ago that she was going to marry Jamie. She knew he wanted to marry her.

Many of the boys who were Jamie's friends used to kid him and say he was "pussy whipped". Jamie only wished it was true. Nothing anyone could say to him could cause him to lose interest in Donna. It wasn't just passion. Jamie was deeply in love with Donna. In December, after Donna graduated from high school, Jamie married Donna. The night before the wedding he lay in bed and asked himself. Do I want to marry Donna just so I can have sex with her. Maybe it wouldn't even be that good. It surely couldn't be as good as the five years of foreplay. It couldn't be as good as the years of fantasies he had about sex with Donna. They were married on a December afternoon the week before Xmas. Donna's parents had given them the choice between a large church wedding or a gift of furniture to start their married life. Like a good Southern woman Donna let Jamie make the choice. Jamie chose the furniture. The wedding was held in the den of Donnas' home with 15 or 20 family members in attendance. It was a nice ceremony followed by a reception from which Jamie was anxious to leave. He had reserved a motel room in a motel next to the Bridge which crosses from Memphis to Arkansas and he proposed to spend their three day honeymoon in this motel room. It was late in the afternoon and cold and rainy by the time Jamie and Donna were able to get away from their wedding reception but neither of them needed the car heater to stay warm. They were both very excited and Jamie found it difficult to keep from breaking the speed limit as they drove to the motel. When they got to the motel room Jamie fought the urge to tear Donnas' clothing off and jump on her. Instead they took a long hot shower together. It was the first time either had seen the other in the nude. Donna looked even better than Jamie had imagined. She was 5-5, weighed 105 pounds and her measurements were 36-19-33. She wore a 36 C bra and her nicely rounded breasts were high and firm. Her nipples were dark brown and looked like prunes. Her complexion was beautiful without any sort of blemish. Her waist was small and she had beautiful thighs and legs. She had just a small sprinkling of brown pubic hair. As they undressed Jamie had an enormous erection which he maintained all the way through their shower. After they dried each other off Jamie picked Donna up and gently took her to bed. He spread her out on the bed and proceeded to kiss her from head to toe. However, when he tried to thrust his erect penis into her he couldn't get it in. Neither of them had previously completed the full sex act but Jamie had read several articles about how things should go. He knew that a woman's hymen was sometimes difficult to penetrate and he didn't want the experience to be painful to Donna. After an anxious hour or so trying to penetrate Donna Jamie stopped for a few minutes and asked Donna if she was hungry. She said she was just a little bit. In truth they were both hungry to complete the sex act. Donna wanted Jamie inside her as much as he wanted to be inside her. Jamie had read that lubrication could sometimes make it easier for a man to break a woman's hymen and he had heard that Vaseline Petroleum jelly was a good thing to use. So he dressed and told Donna he would be right back. He went to a nearby market and bought a jar of petroleum jelly. When he got back to the motel room Donna was still in bed. Jamie slipped into the bathroom and put some petroleum jelly on his penis which was still very much engorged. He slipped back into the bedroom which was now almost completely dark. He found Donnas' mouth with his mouth and thrust his tongue deep into her throat. At the same moment he thrust his fully lubricated penis into Donna and penetrated her hymen. Once he was in he gently moved in and out of Donna. It felt so good that he was afraid he was going to come so each time he felt he was about to come he would slow down. The longer he went the more sounds of pleasure he heard from Donna. They spent most of the night learning about each other. After the first time he had no trouble getting into Donna. Jamie knew from this night on that he had done the right thing. Yes, he thought, getting married just to have sex was the right thing to do. But he knew that what he felt towards Donna wasn't just passion. He cared for her deeply. He wanted to live his life with her. He wanted to make love to her as often as possible but even when they weren't making love he wanted to be with her as much as possible.

Chapter nine-The Villains

During his years as a Saudi Jamie had come to hate Saudis in general and the House of Saud in particular. He believed that they were uniformly evil. He knew that not all Saudis or members of the House of Saud were evil. Some Saudis and some members of the House of Saud tried to lead good and honorable lives. Many believers in Wahhabism focused on the good aspects of their religion and did not support any movement which preached that all non Wahhabis be converted or killed. But these Saudis were in the minority. Over the years Jamie had become fond of the Bedouins. All of them were Moslems but few followed the Wahhabi creed. Most were Sufi which meant that they liked to sing and dance as part of their worship of Allah. The Wahhabis had tried to forcibly convert the Bedouins but it was hard for them to convert a proud and   independent people.

Although Jamie now believed that the House of Saud had financed the attacks on the US he was convinced that they were only the foot soldiers in this war. Nevertheless, he was going to end the reign of the House of Saud and he was going to damage the wealth of Saudi Arabia. He had developed a list of members of the House of Saud who he thought had directly contributed to the attacks including the attack which had killed Jamie's family.

But he also was going after the tip of the pyramid. The person who had developed the plan and made possible the attack which had murdered his family. He knew now who that person was. He knew he would not find him in Saudi Arabia.

The House of Saud and the Saudis were being used by the mastermind behind the attacks. The House of Saud was being told that it was necessary to destroy the United States so that Wahhabism and Saudis could take over the world. This of course was not true. Even

110

with the United States destroyed , the people of the US were only a small portion of the world's people. It was not likely that the people of China and India representing nearly half the world's population would silently sit by and allow the Wahhabist to take over the world.

Jamie had spent many months tracing money to and from Saudi Arabia. He could see that this money was used to pay for the attacks on the U.S. Money is an abstract concept. The Saudis had trillions of dollars in banks all over the world. But the fact of the matter was that this money existed only in theory. If the Saudi had gone into any of the banks with which they banked and asked to withdraw their money the banks would not have been able to deliver currency, gold, diamonds or silver equal to the value of the Saudi deposits. The banks and some governments would have failed and the Saudi deposits would have lost their value. Much of the property the Saudis owned in the United States was now nearly worthless because of the desperate condition the US found its' self in.

Jamie had developed detailed plans on how to destroy the oil wealth of the Saudis.

The Saudis had more than eighty active oil and natural gas fields with more than 1000 working wells. However, more than half of its proven oil reserves were in only eight oil fields. These included Ghawar, the world's largest onshore oil field and Safaniya, the world's largest off shore oil field. Jamie knew it was possible to hit only a few sensitive points "downstream" in the oil system from these eight fields and put the Saudis out of business for at least two years. Another target which Jamie planned to strike was the Abqaig complex, the world's largest oil processing facility. In addition he planned to strike loading terminals at Ras Tanura and Ju'aymah. In addition he would destroy Pump Station Number 1, the station closest to Abqaiq which normally would pump 900,000 barrels of Arabia light and superlight crude per day.

Of greater damage to the House of Saud and to the Saudis Jamie planned to "evaporate" their huge reservoir of bank accounts and shares of stock.. He had detailed information about all of the bank accounts and stock shares held by the House of Saud and their agents.

At the same time he planned to kill more than 300 members of the House of Saud and the House of bin Laden. Having done all of these things Jamie' rage would not yet be sated. He had to kill the person at the top of the pyramid. To do this he would have to go to England.

Chapter Ten-McNamara and Vietnam 1966

After his marriage to Donna the two of them settled into a small second floor apartment near the university Jamie was attending. Jamie went to school from 2 p.m. to 6 p.m. each day and worked from 8 p.m. to 5 a.m. as a Microfilm technician for a real estate title company. He would get home from work about 5:30 a..m., take a bath, make love to Donna and sleep until about noon. After he awoke he would make love to Donna again. He had read the Kama Sutra and liked to try new positions with Donna. He never found a position that he didn't like. On weekends they would often stay in bed for several hours after they awakened and play with each other. Jamie loved the sensuous games he played with Donna. They both won when they played these games. Although they had a small black and white TV they seldom watched it. Jamie often thought to himself that there was nothing on TV as good as Donna. They often said they regretted having waited five years to have sex. Now they were making up for lost time. Unlike some men Jamie didn't have nights out with the boys. Many of his friends thought Jamie had moved away from Memphis because he never saw them. Their first year of marriage went by very quickly. After that first night Jamie didn't have to use Vaseline.

To celebrate their first anniversary they went to dinner at a nice night club. With dinner Jamie ordered a cold bottle of Moet Chandon Champaigne. Jamie was a teetotaler but had a glass of the champagne anyway. Donna liked champagne and she drank the rest of the bottle. The night club had a dance floor and Jamie enjoyed very much escorting Donna around the floor. She was wearing a beautiful red dress he had bought her as an anniversary present and she looked very beautiful. Other men eyed Jamie enviously. Jamie was thrilled when he realized that when they got home he would get to remove this red dress from Donna and that he would be able to take off her bra and her panties. By the time they left the night club Donna was a little bit giggly from the champagne and Jamie had an enormous erection. When they got home he slowly removed Donna's dress, her bra and her panties. It seemed to Jamie that he had never before gotten into Donna so deeply. It was a wonderful night. He thrust from many angles and his penis seemed to slide in so easily compared to their honeymoon night. When Jamie would tire Donna would get on top and sit astride his penis and pump up and down. It was such a beautiful sight to look up at her with her breasts swaying up and down with the movement of her hips and her beautiful face aglow with pleasure. It was at times like this that Jamie would have liked to stay suspended for eternity. He couldn't imagine anything in life which could be better than these times.

Nine months later, after an easy and uneventful pregnancy their first child, a daughter, Cindy, was born. Like her mother Cindy was beautiful. Like her father she had blue eyes and by her first birthday she had a head of curly blond hair. The new baby didn't change Jamie and Donna's sex life. It continued to be an important part of their life interrupted with diaper changes and nocturnal feedings. Often when the baby had to nurse in the middle of the night they would make love once the baby was fed and back to sleep. After Jamie graduated from college he came to a crossroads in his life. He had many job offers. One of the most intriguing came from the U.S. Army. The Vietnam War was taking more and more resources from the United States. Jamie was politically naïve and accepted the government position on the war without much personal research. Robert McNamara was the genius installed By Lyndon Johnson to run the Department of Defense and McNamara was looking for what he called whiz kids. On a whim Jamie had taken what the government called the Federal Service Entrance Examination. It had been given to 4000 people in numerous locations throughout the country. Jamie liked standardized examinations and he scored the highest of the 4000 who took the exam. He received a personal invitation to come to Washington, D.C. to be interviewed by McNamara's team. Those being interviewed were impressive. The group was dominated by graduates of Harvard, Princeton, Yale, Stanford and other top level colleges. Most had not taken the FSEE but had been invited to be interviewed because they had finished at the top of their college classes. Jamie wasn't overshadowed by this group of scholars. In fact during the interview with McNamara he stood out from the others. McNamara liked him immediately and invited him to have dinner with he and his wife at a nice Georgetown restaurant. Jamie had brought Donna and Cindy to D.C. with him and he told McNamara that he would come if he could find a babysitter. McNamara told Jamie bring the baby with you. When Jamie, Donna and Cindy arrived at the restaurant to have dinner with the McNamara's everyone in the restaurant stopped to watch them as they came in. It wasn't because of Robert McNamara that the other diners stared. It was because of Donna and Cindy. They were a beautiful pair. Donna was dressed in a conservative white wool dress and her beautiful skin created a wonderful contrast with the dress. Cindy was dressed in a pink dress and her blond hair and blue eyes would have looked good in any setting.

McNamara hired Jamie as an Inventory Management Analyst and assigned him to work in a small office deep in the bowels of the Pentagon. Jamie rented a small house, on a quiet, tree lined street in Arlington, a few minutes from the Pentagon, and in late 1965 moved Donna and Cindy into the home. By early 1966 Jamie was deeply immersed in his job at the Pentagon. Donna was also pregnant. Jamie knew when conception had taken place. McNamara had sent him to look at a helicopter factory in Connecticut and Jamie had been away from Donna and Cindy for a week. It was the first time they had been apart during their marriage. The night of the day he returned was like a second honeymoon. After they had put Cindy to bed Jamie had taken a bath and was lying in bed waiting for Donna. After she finished her bath she changed into a bikini outfit with a leopard pattern. The panties and top just barely covered Donna and, as usual, she looked beautiful. Jamie never tired of looking at Donna. She was getting more beautiful as time went by. Her waist and hips remained slender and her complexion was remarkable. That night he knew that he had sent into Donna enough sperm to father a hundred children. Afterwards as they lay on the bed Donna told him about an incident that had happened while he was gone. One evening, after Donna had put Cindy to bed she had taken a shower. As she stepped from the bathroom into the bedroom, wrapped in a towel, she was confronted by a large, naked black man who had broken a lock to get into the house. Apparently he realized that there was a woman taking a bath so he had stripped naked. Donna was so startled when she saw him that she dropped her towel and stood their naked. She didn't scream. The man was equally startled when he saw how beautiful Donna was. He must have thought that this was his lucky day. He immediately got an enormous erection which was pointed directly at Donna. His intentions were obvious as he moved forward to push Donna onto the bed. Suddenly her foot shot forward as she buried her foot deep into his groin. He let out a scream of pain and bent over to grab his scrotum. As he did so Donna hit him in the Adam's apple with the palm of one hand and on the right side of his head with the other hand. The man was unconscious before he hit the floor. Donna immediately hog tied the man to the foot of the bed, dressed and called the police. The police came and removed the unfortunate man. Donna was grateful to Jamie for the karate lessons he had enrolled her in many years ago. They had become interested in karate during a conversation with Elvis at one of his parties. Donna was an excellent student. She didn't tell Jamie about the incident until he got home. When she did he was badly shaken and the next day he found them an apartment in a very secure complex favored by other Pentagon employees. Jamie's work at the Pentagon was pretty routine. His job was to analyze computer generated reports to determine how many helicopters parts should be ordered to provide maintenance for a particular helicopter, the CH-54 Flying Crane, during combat operations in Vietnam. The conditions in Vietnam were substantially different than the test conditions the manufacturer of the helicopters had used to determine parts replacement schedules. Vietnam was hot and muggy and often the helicopters would fly into very dusty conditions. Jamie didn't work directly for McNamara but occasionally McNamara would come by to run an idea by Jamie. It often was a thought that had nothing to do with Jamie's department. Jamie was one of the minds that McNamara liked to use when he was trying to make a decision. Furthermore McNamara enjoyed coming by Jamie's office to get a look at the large photo of Donna that Jamie kept on his desk. McNamara, although happily married, liked beautiful women and Donna was very beautiful. During the middle of Donna's pregnancy Jamie was asked to go to Vietnam to perform what the Army called a Parts Provisioning Pipeline study. He was asked to be there for 11 weeks. Jamie went home and told Donna that Secretary McNamara wanted Jamie to go to South Vietnam for 11 weeks. As a civilian he would be carrying a calculator and sets of computer printouts. Donna was three months pregnant and would be six months pregnant by the time Jamie was scheduled to return. Donna immediately told Jamie he should go. They agreed that Donna and Cindy would go back to Memphis and stay with her parents while Jamie was gone. Her parents would really enjoy having Donna and Cindy visit them while Jamie was gone.

Jamie was to conduct a study whereby he would travel with spare parts and a couple of mainframes for the Army's largest helicopter, the CH-54 Flying Crane from where they were manufactured to the maintenance or storage depot where they would be used or stored in Vietnam. The Army had been having trouble keeping up with some of the more expensive helicopter components. Several engines which cost $225,000. each to make, and which had a scrap metal value of about $600., had disappeared between the factory in the U.S. and the destination bases in Vietnam. Jamie's job was to keep track of the parts and document how they were handled. To track and document the chain of custody.

Jamie and the helicopter spare parts left an airbase in Connecticut one early morning in a huge transport aircraft. Unlike a commercial jet the transport plane would fly a bit slower and would have to land more often to re-fuel. It had a comfortable jump seat which gave Jamie plenty of room to stretch out. The big plane stopped in Alaska, Hawaii, Samoa and Korea before arriving at Tan Son Nhut airbase just outside Saigon. At that time the airbase at Tan Son Nhut was the busiest airbase in the world. It was surrounded by hundreds of acres of storage areas containing ammunition, firearms, tanks, trucks, jeeps, artillery pieces, cases of Busch Beer, bottles of Jack Daniels and all the other things an army needed to fight a war. Tan Son Nhut looked like a giant ant hill with ants scurrying everywhere. Pulling, hauling, transporting, pushing, towing. Huge olive drab cement trucks sat in rows ready to move concrete to build runways, bridges and roads for the war. Bicycles and motorbikes mixed in with the military traffic and MP's kept everything moving.

Before leaving the Pentagon Jamie had been promoted to GS-12 making him the youngest Government Service employee at the 12 rating in the federal government. He had started his job as a GS-7 just short of a year ago. His government rating made him the equivalent of a regular Army Lt. Colonel which, even for a civilian, was important in terms of where he would be housed and how he would be transported. From Tan Son Nhut Jamie was driven by a regular army Sergeant by jeep into central Saigon to an old French hotel, the Star

Hotel, which was to be his home while he was in Vietnam.

The hotel had been built by the French more than 50 years

earlier and its original elegance was now a bit frayed. The

front lobby contained a long wooden counter where new

arrivals could check in. Three large ceiling fans whirred

around in the lobby trying to circulate the cool air

conditioned air. A number of people sat in large comfortable

chairs pretending to read newspapers while they monitored

all the new arrivals. The Hotel's guests came from all over

the world but most were French, English or American. Many

of them worked for companies which were serving the

military. Some of them were CIA agents pretending to be

something other than spies. After his arrival in Saigon Jamie

had two days before he had to report for his assignment. He

checked into his hotel, into a comfortable room with high

ceilings and a ceiling fan to circulate the air conditioned air.

The room was on the third

floor and had a third floor balcony overlooking the busy area around the hotel. After checking into his room Jamie took a long shower and changed into the comfortable clothing he had brought with him. He put on a loose fitting casual short and a new pair of well tailored white slacks he had bought in Memphis. The first evening Jamie ate dinner at the hotel's old and elegant restaurant which was mostly patronized by Westerners. Few Vietnamese came to it. The food was cheap and very good and the service was excellent. After dinner, Jamie adjourned to a reading room just off of the hotel lobby and was reading a recent edition of the International Herald Tribune. A young man approached Jamie and asked if he was new at the hotel. He asked other questions which Jamie felt free to answer. The young man, whose name was Victor, worked for the British embassy and had been there for a month. He explained to Jamie that if he chose to do so he could hire a beautiful young Vietnamese girl to take care of him during his stay at the hotel. The girl would live in the room with Jamie, take care of keeping the room clean, do his laundry, and do whatever else Jamie needed to have done. The young man lingered when he said "whatever else".

He said he would be glad to take Jamie to a place where he could select a young girl. Jamie thanked the young man and declined his assistance. Victor, said quickly that if Jamie would prefer to have a young boy that could also be arranged. Jamie laughed and again thanked Victor and waived his wedding ring in front of him and explained that if he did have a young girl living with him his wife might not like it. He pulled a photo of Donna from his wallet to show to Victor. Victor whistled softly when he saw the photo. Jamie also told Victor that even though he would be staying at the hotel for 11 weeks most of the time he would be riding around the country in helicopters with his clipboard and calculator. The next morning Jamie left the hotel to walk around the neighborhood.

He was dressed casually and comfortably for the heat and humidity of Saigon and it was still cool in the morning when he started his walk. He had a wide brimmed fashionable Panama hat covering his red hair which he hoped would shield his face from the rays of the fierce Saigon sun. Except for the khaki clad soldiers and the big military trucks traveling through the streets it was difficult to believe that Saigon was in a country at war. Saffron clad Buddhist monks moved through the streets carrying the vestments of their calling. School children dressed neatly in the uniforms of the Catholic schools the French had left behind walked to and from school chattering as all school children are prone to do. He wondered what the school children thought about the many Westerners who they passed on the street. About men like Jamie or men like the young soldiers dressed neatly in khaki. Jamie did not feel threatened by the Vietnamese who passed him on the street. Many of the children smiled and giggled as they passed him on the street. Businessmen dressed in white, light weight suits carrying briefcases went from money making opportunity to money making opportunity. Peugeots, Citroens, Mercedes, motorbikes and bicycles mixed together in the crowded streets. The war had made thousands of people into prostitutes, pimps or smugglers to feed the war machine. Many Vietnamese worked in the city by day and by night served the fight for independence.

Jamie's hotel was in Cholon, the Chinese section of Saigon, and Jamie liked the hustle and bustle of the area. At lunch he ate at a beautiful Vietnamese restaurant underneath a large Banyan Tree. He had a couple of Spring Rolls and some of the delicious Pho noodle soup. It was difficult to believe that Saigon was the capitol of a city of a country at war. Only in areas with a lot of G-I friendly bars did you see many men in uniform. In most of Saigon life seemed normal. Buses and taxis carried people throughout the city. Saigon had the bustle of a city being enriched by billions of dollars from the war. The city fascinated Jamie. It was very alive. Beautiful young women in traditional dress and in modern dress gave Jamie's eyes a treat. He thought the Vietnamese women were beautiful. They moved with a grace he had never seen in an American woman. Their long straight black hair gleamed and bounced as they walked down the crowded streets. The area around his hotel was packed with French bakeries, restaurants and carts selling many different things. He could see and smell the stacks of hot bread stacked in bakery windows. He could smell the tantalizing aroma of many different restaurants anytime he walked the streets near his hotel. On the afternoon of his first day in Saigon Jamie went by the U.S. Embassy to register. It was a busy place with long lines of people waiting in line to apply for travel visas. The lines were orderly and quiet. Jamie didn't like to jump a line so he got in line with everyone else. One of the Embassy attendants asked Jamie if he was an American and when Jamie replied yes the attendant told him he didn't need to wait in line with the others. He was directed through the cool halls of the massive building to the consular section. He displayed his American passport and his Army Aviation Materiel Command I.D.. His photo was taken and he was quickly issued a little blue card on which was his photo tightly laminated with the seal of the US State Department across the face of the I.D. Carry this with you at all times he was told. A pleasant young man had interviewed him for a few moments and had given Jamie a packet of materials which warned him about pick pockets, mosquitoes, prostitutes, venereal diseases, drinking water, T.B., drug usage and "the enemy".

To prepare his report Jamie followed the parts and main frame items, with which he had ridden more than 12000 miles, to the storage facility at Tan Son Nhut where they were stored in large Quonset huts. He carefully reviewed the procedures in place to account for and store these parts which included engines, fuel controls and thousands of bits and pieces. He reviewed the procedure being used to account for items which were sent from the warehouse out to the field for storage or for installation into a helicopter. He reviewed the inventory controls at the warehouse. The next day he rode in a big helicopter, a CH46, which was used to transport parts out to bases in the countryside and he documented what happened when a particular part reached its destination. He watched as some parts were actually installed into a helicopter and he noted deficiencies and made changes on the spot to the procedures which were in place. He needed to make sure that there was a chain of custody which would make it possible to trace what happened to a part once it reached Vietnam. During the next three weeks he traveled all over Vietnam and visited 46 different bases. He issued many changes to the system used to keep track of parts. He felt like an outsider when he talked with some of the soldiers he met. He knew that if the war had been at its' present stage when he was 19 or 20 that he would have probably been there as a combat soldier and would be carrying a gun instead of a clipboard and an abacus. He knew that many men avoided being drafted by claiming homosexuality, flat feet, bad backs or conscientious believer status. Jamie knew that if the war had been at its' present stage when he was 18 he would probably have enlisted. About the only thing which would have kept him from doing so was the fear of leaving Donna alone in Memphis. Part of Jamie was Tennessean. It was the birthplace of his mother and the summers around his maternal grandfather, J.R. had imbued Jamie with many of the characteristics of a Tennessean. Tennessee is known as the "Volunteer" state because in war time Tennesseans traditionally served their country or state. It was Tennessee which had sent Andy Jackson to fight the British in New Orleans, Davy Crockett to fight the Mexicans at the

Alamo, Alvin York to fight the Germans in Europe. Sergeant York was from the same part of Tennessee as Jamie's grandfather, J.R. York had won the Congressional Medal of Honor in WW I and was the most decorated U.S. soldier from that War. Jamie felt lucky that he was 26 and married rather than 18 or 19 and single. To some extent he felt cheated of a chance to show his valor. As a boy he had seen a movie about the Korean War called "Pork Chop Hill" and he had tried to calculate the chances of being drafted to serve in a war like that one. His older cousin, Bobby, had been the only survivor in his Army Platoon when the Chinese Army had overrun the U.S. military on the Inchon Peninsula. Jamie knew, if he had been drafted and asked to fight in a war that he would have done so. Not because of a feeling of patriotism but of a fear of being labeled a coward or a shirker. He knew that was what brought many American G.I's to Vietnam to die.

Jamie didn't see any of the combat which could spring up at any time in any place in the countryside as he went about preparing his report.. In fact he had been ordered to stay away from bases which were considered "hot" spots. He did see many different signs that a war was being fought. On one occasion his helicopter which flew in spare parts flew back out with body bags containing dead G.I.'s Each bag had attached to it dog tags identifying the dead G.I. Once back at Tan Son Nhut Jamie had seen the metal tubes which were used to ship dead G.I's back to the U.S. for burial. During the trips Jamie took out to storage and maintenance base camps he saw more of the war than he wanted to see.

After six weeks in Vietnam Jamie received 10 days of R & R during which he could take a vacation in the area or he could travel to Bangkok. He elected to stay in Vietnam. While out in the field just before his R & R was scheduled to begin Jamie had visited with one of his cousins. His cousin Joe was from his maternal grandmothers Cherokee Indian tribe in East Tennessee. He was a staff sergeant and knowing that Jamie was about to have a ten day leave Joe asked Jamie if he was like to go out on a long range recon patrol with Joe and his nine man squad. The squad would be flown by helicopter to a mountain ridge deep in one of the jungles near the border with Cambodia. The squad had been on this particular mission before and, as Joe's cousin described it was like a camping trip. The squad would set up an observation post on a mountain ridge and observe movement of enemy troops and supplies being moved along a mountain road in a valley ten miles away. The squad had been to this observation post in the jungle twice before. They had instructions to maintain radio silence, not to have any visible smoke during the day and not to engage the enemy. Joe described the jungle to Jamie and how interesting it was. It would be against Army regulations for Jamie to tag along on this patrol which was scheduled to last three days but in this part of Vietnam Army regulations were not always followed so Jamie agreed to spend part of his R & R on this patrol. Just before the squad was ready to get on the helicopter to be flown to the observation post Joe gave Jamie a typical pack containing his "camping" supplies. This included a small pup tent, mosquito netting, a sharp hunting knife, some Meals Ready to Eat, some bottles of Skin So Soft to repel mosquitoes and a few other survival items. Joe also had a M-1 Carbine issued to Jamie. At age 14 Jamie had spent a summer on the reservation with Joe's family, in the Smokey Mountains and Joe remembered that Jamie was a real sharpshooter. As he gave Jamie the carbine he assured him he wouldn't have to use it. The helicopter flew out from the main base very early in the morning and it flew high in the air until it got near the observation post high on a mountain ridge. After the helicopter landed in a small clearing which had previously been hacked out of the forest the men began making their observation post comfortable. They dug a few latrines and set up a shower area near a mountain spring they had discovered during previous trips. It was a beautiful jungle area and Jamie was glad he had come. He set up his tent and covered his sleeping area with mosquito netting and went for a walk around the area. The Jungle was thick and green and Jamie was careful not to get too far from the camp. The giant trees provided cool shade and the mountain air felt good. The big trees kept much sunlight from reaching the jungle floor and prevented undergrowth from growing on the floor of the jungle. Jamie could hear all the jungle noises. He enjoyed them all. Monkeys chattered in the trees. There was a shallow mountain stream from which Jamie was able to catch fish which he took back to the camp and ate raw. The fish were delicious and Jamie found some wild onions to eat with them. He also found some wild berries. The night was really wonderful. The mosquitoes weren't as bad as Jamie had expected but the ones that buzzed around him seemed as big as Hummingbirds. The night jungle had lots of noises and the squad thought that they had heard a tiger. In a previous trip they had spotted a tiger. That could have been a problem since they weren't allowed to fire their weapons. Just in case he encountered a tiger Jamie made himself a spear. His cousin had also brought with him a cross bow which had been given to him by a Montengard villager a month earlier. The three days at the observation post went by quickly. Jamie loved the Jungle. He had spent his 14th and 15th summers with Joe's family on the Cherokee Reservation in the East Tennessee Mountains. Joe's grandfather was Jamie's maternal grandmother's brother. There were three Joes in the family. Old Joe was Jamie's great uncle. Big Joe was his son and little Joe was the cousin who had enticed Jamie to come on this Jungle trip. During his two summers on the reservation Jamie's many cousins had taught him to survive in the remote mountains of the reservation. They had taught him what could be eaten. How to fish and to trap rabbits with hand made snares. On his 15th birthday Big Joe had taken Jamie out into the middle of the Mountains and left him to find his way back home. It was a test to see if he was old enough to be considered a man. He was given some fish hooks, fishing line, a hunting knife, a flint, some canvas, a canteen and a few other items. He had been taught how to determine direction and he knew very well how to survive in the mountains. During his way back he caught fish in mountain streams ate wild vegetables and fruit he found growing abundantly in the mountains, gone up a tree to get away from a wild boar, had chased away a curious black bear and made it back home in only two days. Most boys took three or four days. So Jamie was at home in the Jungle. The squad was expecting the helicopter to arrive at a specified time to pick them up and so they all waited at the clearing where they expected the helicopter to land. No helicopter arrived. Joe, as squad leader, had been told not to use his radio. By the next day, the men in the squad were getting worried. All the squad members were kids in their late teens and early 20's and Joe and Jamie were the oldest in the group. After the helicopter didn't show up Joe asked Jamie what he thought they should do. Jamie said they should walk back to the camp. Although the squad had detailed maps of the area it was 55 miles back to the camp which can be a long way in a jungle. Their maps reflected the route back to the camp which included crossing a couple of small rivers. There were also several villages along the way and the squad had no way of knowing if the villagers were friendly or not. They also didn't know if they might encounter VC or North Vietnamese regulars. After a long conversation with Jamie, Joe told the squad they were going to walk back to their base. They left a message attached to a tree in the clearing telling any helicopter that did come for them where they had gone. They immediately began the walk back. First they had to go down from the mountain and along a dry creek bed. The first night they camped under a large tree full of monkeys. They didn't start a fire for fear that someone in the area would smell the smoke. 55 miles is not a long distance for young soldiers to walk if the walk is down a long straight road. However, the valley they were in didn't have a road. They did find a path which led in the right direction but they were afraid of what they would find along the path. They reached the first river they needed to cross in the middle of the second day of their hike. One of the soldiers swam with a rope to the other side and hooked up the rope to a tree. The men were able to use the rope to send over their clothing and their back packs with their weapons and supplies. Each man stripped naked and swam the river. Once on the other side they dried themselves and put their boots and clothing back on. They continued to follow the path until they came to a small village. The village was at the bottom of a small hill and so they had spotted it from several hundred yards away. It was a small village with no more than ten thatched roof cottages and a small clearing. They watched the village closely for an hour to see if any of the villagers looked like soldiers. It looked like an ordinary farm village. Jamie agreed to go ahead first. He slowly approached the village and as he came to the first house an elderly woman came out to welcome him. In a few minutes most of the villagers were shaking his hand. They seemed friendly. They had not seen an American before. Jamie beckoned the other members of the squad to come down. They spent the night in the village and the Villagers cooked them a nice meal. They also gave the villagers some of their MRE's and explained what they were doing in the area. They told the villagers they were lost and trying to make there way back to their camp.. The next morning two of the Villagers guided the squad to the next river and showed them where a boat was which they used for the crossing. The rest of the hike was fairly routine and as they got closer to their base they could see helicopters going and coming from the base. When they got to the perimeter of the base they were careful to identify themselves. Once they checked in with their unit they learned that the helicopter which had taken them to their observation post had never returned to the base. Either it had been shot down or had crashed because of mechanical problems. The base thought the helicopter had crashed taking Joe and the squad to there post so they had been presumed lost. Jamie had enjoyed the camping trip with his cousin but he now realized how close he and Joe had come to being in real trouble. Joe could have been court marshaled and thrown in the brig for taking Jamie on this LURP. (Long Range Recon Patrol) Jamie could have been sent back to the U.S.

Jamie reported back to Tan Son Nhut to resume gathering material for his Report. His first day back he rode out to a base which performed maintenance and repairs to Army helicopters. This trip was on a Huey One, the most common helicopter used in Vietnam. Hueys were used to launch rockets on enemy positions or as a platform to fire 50 caliber machine guns. The Huey was the Army's work horse. For the First Air Cavalry the Huey had replaced the horse. Jamie had been instructed to stay away from "hot" landing zones but when he rode in a helicopter he always sat on a helmet as the helicopter would come in low to land. This particular trip, unlike the many others he had taken, would be different. He could tell that the crew was tense as they came into land. One of the crew pointed to a column of smoke in the distance. He could see Hueys taking off from the base. One of the members of the crew in the helicopter in which he was riding pointed towards the smoke and said that "Charlie" was getting his butt kicked. Jamie was used to this sort of bravado. The remark reminded Jamie of many locker rooms he had been in before a football game. He knew that if Charlie, the Viet Cong, was getting his butt kicked that those who were doing the kicking would end up with sore feet. As they

landed Jamie could see that the field hospital at the base was

very busy and he knew that G.I's were getting more than just

sore feet. Men, on both sides of the battle, were dying. The

base had only one of the big CH-54's that Jamie's group was

assigned to. The CH-54 could be used to retrieve Hueys

which had been shot down. Jamie could see a junk yard

which contained half a dozen wrecked Hueys. He wondered

how the crews of these helicopters had fared. From the looks

of the wrecked helicopters he knew the crews had not done

well. That evening Jamie sat around a tent with some of the

G.I's who had been in the battle that day. Nine G.I's had

been killed and 21 wounded during the battle. The men were

exhausted but strangely animated. Some of them were

smoking the strong marijuana which seemed to be

everywhere in Vietnam. The next day he rode back to Saigon

in a big CH-46 transport helicopter containing the bodies, or

what was left of them, of the

men who had been killed in the battle the day before. Jamie knew these men had been alive when they boarded Hueys for the battle of the previous day. He knew that these men had not wanted to die and that they had left behind people who loved them. Mothers, Fathers, brothers, sisters, wives, children, friends. He knew these men had left behind girlfriends, family dogs or baseball gloves. He knew that some of them had left behind prized cars or pickup trucks stored in garages or barns. The Army would send two people out to notify the families or other next of kin . It was always the visit no one wanted to make or receive. The dead G.I.'s families would see them or their coffins one more time. After the funeral the deceased's possessions would have to be given away. The survivors would have to apply for the G.I. life insurance benefit. Jamie knew that these men had just begun to live. Most were under the age of 25 and many were 18 or 19. Some were as young as 17. Some had lied about their ages to join the military. For many of them their first and last sexual experience had been with a Vietnamese girl in a brothel in Saigon. Some had left behind pregnant wives who would bear children who would never know a father except through letters and photographs. Jamie had seen these men, or ones like them, coming off of commercial airliners at Tan Son Nhut squinting in the hot sun as they walked to transport trucks. The men in the body bags were Jacks, Jims, Bills or Petes from small towns, farms or big cities. He knew that none had expected to die in Vietnam. Some had died quickly without knowing who or what had killed them. Some had remained conscious from a mortal wound and had died slowly and painfully. Some had been killed by enemy fire and some had been killed by friendly fire.

It was all beginning to seem so senseless to Jamie. After Jamie returned to Saigon he received an invitation to attend a cocktail party at the British Embassy and he decided to attend. The British embassy in Saigon was in an area of the city which had previously been a neighborhood of wealthy French colonialists. It was lined with huge Banyan and Monkey Pod trees which provided shade and relative coolness in the heat and humidity of Saigon. Jamie didn't have an extensive wardrobe. He wore a white sports coat and a pair of dark slacks which made him look a bit out of place among the other guests most of whom were dressed as if they had just stepped out of the Vietnamese version of Vogue Magazine.

He had been invited by Victor who Jamie had bumped into just after returning to his hotel after the camping trip with Little Joe. It was a quiet cocktail party with clumps of people standing around with glasses in hand taking an occasional canapé from the trays being circulated throughout the crowd by servers dressed in white jackets. Except for the fact that he had red hair, blue eyes and was more than 6-1, Jamie might have been mistaken for one of the servers. Normally at something like this back in

D.C. Jamie would have had in his hand a glass of ice over which he would pour a coke. However, since this cocktail party was being given by the British no ice was to be found. Finally he found a glass of ginger ale to occupy his hand. Victor introduced him around and Jamie found himself talking to a Vietnamese man who looked to be in his 30's. The man's English was nearly perfect. His name was Troung. He told Jamie that he had attended Ohio State University and that he still followed the fortunes of Ohio State football. He was dressed in what looked like a tailor made light gray suit and had an expensive looking watch on his wrist. He told Jamie that he had been born in the Mekong Delta and had been schooled in France and in England. The man worked for a Vietnamese company which was helping to provide supplies to the U.S. military. During the conversation Jamie learned that the man had three children, sons aged 19 and 22 and a daughter age 16. All three of the children were going to school in France. It was a pleasant evening for Jamie with small talk with a number of interesting people. However, the conversation with the Vietnamese man stuck in Jamie's mind. The man had said his two sons were going to school in France. This meant, of course, that they were safe from the war. This stuck in Jamie's mind and he thought about it over and over. He had ridden with body bags containing young G.I's many of whom were probably the same ages as this man's sons. None of these dead G.I's would ever get a chance to go to school in France. Some of them had volunteered for military service but many were drafted by the army. They had struggled to survive the rigors of basic training. The dirt and the mud, the barbed wire, the weapons training and the pungent smell of cordite and gun powder. They had all said goodbyes to someone- to wives, girlfriends, mothers, fathers, brothers, sisters, friends, old dogs, favorite cars or motorcycles. "Take care of yourself"- "be careful"- they all had been told. Why were these man's sons not serving in the South Vietnamese army. Didn't they or there father want to help defend their own country. Many Americans were doing so and many were dying. The conversation with Mr. Truong had given Jamie more to think about.

A few days later Jamie was invited to take part in a demonstration of the CH-54 Flying Crane, the helicopter which his Parts Provisioning Pipeline Study was supporting. The CH-54 was the largest helicopter in the Army's fleet of aircraft. As a lift helicopter it could lift any other Army aircraft including another CH-54 without its' rotors. The CH-54 could lift a jeep or an artillery field piece. It could carry a field hospital pod, fully equipped with an operating room out to the field and detach it on the ground. The Army was going to put on a demonstration of the CH-54 for an assembled group of visiting congressmen and for some members of the media. The aircraft usually carried a pilot and a co-pilot and a crane operator and assistant.

Jamie was asked to sit in as the assistant. The demonstration was to be simple. The CH-54 would hover over an artillery field piece, the crane operator would hook a cable onto the field piece and the helicopter would fly the heavy field piece from one side of the field to the other and sit it down gently. At least that was how the demonstration should have proceeded. However, after the crane operator had hooked onto the field piece when the helicopter went up to lift instead of the field piece going up the helicopter came down. It all happened so quickly that Jamie didn't have time to be afraid. One moment he was sitting in the helicopter and the next moment the helicopter had crashed in a cloud of dust and had broken apart. Jamie found himself in a pile of brush. He had strong pain in his neck and shoulder and he could smell jet fuel soaking the pile of brush. The crane operator lay next to him unconscious. They were both still strapped in their seats. Jamie realized that he was hurt but he also realized that he was alive and that he needed to get away from the pile of brush soaked in highly combustible jet fuel before a spark set it afire.. He unloosened his seat belt and that of the crane operator and dragged himself and the crane operator away from the pile of brush as an ambulance came rushing up to the scene and nearly ran over them. The two of them were strapped onto the skids of a Huey One and taken to a nearby base hospital. Jamie never lost consciousness and because of the pain he was feeling wasn't surprised when he was told at the hospital that he had a broken collarbone and a broken shoulder. The Crane Operator had two broken legs and a badly broken arm. The investigation which followed the crash determined that it was caused by pilot error. The pilot had not built up enough torque before trying to lift the field piece. The Army investigation revealed that the pilot had been out drinking the night before and had less than 3 hours of sleep before the accident. The pilot would probably have been court marshaled except for one small detail. He had been killed in the crash. The co-pilot had

suffered a broken back and a broken jaw.

Jamie remained in the field hospital for a day before being

transferred to an Army hospital in Saigon. While he

recovered he did a lot of reading about the history of

Vietnam. The hospital was next to the U.S. Embassy which

had an excellent library. Before coming to Vietnam Jamie

had not studied much about the country. He accepted the

official government position that the U.S. was in Vietnam to

protect the country from being over run by Communists.

Some in government had discussed what had become known

as the domino theory. Jamie learned that the same Viet Cong

the U.S. was now fighting had fought with U.S. troops

against the Japanese during World War II. After the war Ho

Chi Minh sought to drive the French from Vietnam so that an

independent Vietnam could be established. In the siege and

the battle at Dien Bien Phu, the forces of Ho Chi Minh had

badly defeated the French

and persuaded the French to leave the country. An international conference was held in Geneva in which France, England and the Vietnamese independence movement, the Viet Minh, led by Ho Chi Minh, agreed that free elections should be held in Vietnam in 1957 so that the people of Vietnam could decide who would rule them. Dwight Eisenhower was President of the United States and the U.S. State Department and the CIA told Eisenhower that Ho Chi Minh would be elected President of Vietnam if the election was held. To Eisenhower and Dean Acheson, his Secretary of State, the thought of having another communist government in S.E. Asia was not appealing. Some even argued what they called the "domino theory". China already had a communist government. If Vietnam became a communist nation it might unite with China and force the other Asian nations in the area to follow suit. Thailand, Laos, Cambodia, Burma would be part of a chain of dominos. The trouble with this theory, according to what Jamie read, was that Vietnam and China were bitter enemies and had been for centuries. During his time in Saigon Jamie had already gotten a long look at the corruption which pervaded the South Vietnamese government. He knew that many wealthy Vietnamese sent their own children to safety in France while Americans died in battles, to "save" the country. He also knew that many Vietnamese and for that matter, many Americans, were profiting from the war. The more he read the more Jamie was convinced that the U.S. had wrongly interfered in what was basically a civil war. Towards the end of his TDY in Vietnam Jamie experienced one other thing which affected how he thought about the war. He was on his way to a base a couple of hundred miles out from Saigon. The helicopter landed in an area which had shortly before been hit by rockets from U.S. helicopters. An Army officer was doing a body count of the dead enemy. In the pile of bodies was the body of a little girl who looked to be about six years of age. She was dressed in her catholic school uniform and still was clutching a book bag in her hand. She looked like she was sleeping. She had a pink ribbon around the black hair which was piled on top of her hair. Near her was an older child, a boy about 8, who was also dressed in a school uniform. He looked like he may have been the little girl's brother and from the position of his body he may have been trying to protect the little girl. Jamie looked at the scene and he noticed that the officer doing the body count included the bodies of the two children in the count. This was probably the turning point for Jamie.

He knew that the military placed great importance on these body counts and that after the body counts were done the bodies would be pushed into a mass grave and forgotten with no attempt made to identify the dead. He knew that many Vietnamese sons and daughter who had become "Charlie's" died, and as far as their families were concerned, simply disappeared. Jamie had heard young soldiers talking about villages they had destroyed. Whole villages strafed, bombed and napalmed leaving nothing but ashes where once had been thatched roof houses of farmers tending rice and banana plants. Pigs and water buffalo burned to a crisp. Babes in arms, pregnant women, toddlers with looks of wonder on their faces as they died. Whole families-mothers, fathers, brothers, sisters, aunts, uncles, old men, old women. Sometimes the attacks were ordered by South Vietnamese bureaucrats trying to make an example of a particular village. Sometimes an attack would be made against an entire village because it was thought that one young man or young woman had left the village to join the v.c. Yes the fight for "freedom" proceeded on but Jamie had begun to wonder whose freedom was really at stake. His opinions about the war had changed drastically. It was no longer parades and flags blowing in the wind. It was no longer about politicians talking about "dominoes". Now it was body bags and dead 18 year olds and three gun salutes in Keokuk, Iowa. It was babes in arms burnt to a crisp. Young school girls clad in parochial school uniforms lying dead in the heat. It was Mr. Phuong and his Parisian sons. These were the images Jamie had when thinking about the War.

When Jamie returned to Washington, D.C. He completed his report and submitted it to his superior. Shortly afterwards he submitted his resignation. Secretary McNamara came by to try to talk Jamie out of leaving. Jamie didn't tell McNamara what he had seen and learned in Vietnam. He didn't tell him that he could not in good conscience continue to do any thing that supported the war.

Chapter 11-The Lord who was a banker

In 1933, Germany, under the Dictatorial Rule of Adolph Hitler and his Third Reich, sought to conquer the world and establish a single world government. Under such a world government, which the Germans sought to rule as the "*Master Race*", the Third

Reich sought to improve the world with German "efficiency". They proposed to eliminate those who they perceived as weak, as they did during their rule in Germany. This would involve murdering people with physical or mental defects and others the German perceived as inferior. This included Gypsies, Jews, Communists and many other categories of people the Germans considered "unworthy". It would include babies born with defects, children with disabling diseases, those with mental illnesses- all those who didn't match up to the German ideal of perfection. A very harsh world in which differences between people would be eliminated even if it was necessary to eliminate a lot of people. The Germans planned to establish a world government which would eliminate political, tribal, religious and cultural conflicts. With this new world government, as proposed by the Germans of the Third Reich, the "Master Race" would rule all those considered inferior. They believed that a world free of conflict

162

and free of those deemed inferior would be a better world with plentiful food and water for the remaining favored few. They saw an end to famine and disease to be made possible by the efficiencies imposed by the Third Reich and by those inferiors they planned to enslave.

Jamie was in favor of a world government but not one created by the harsh, cruel methods which had been proposed by the Third Reich. Like the words of the song by the Beetles "Imagine", Jamie could imagine that the world would be a better place without religion, property and the other things which tend to divide people and cause strife. He also knew that many Americans feared the creation of a world government because they believed that a world government would "spread the wealth" and it was American wealth which would be spread. Americans were selfish and didn't want to share their wealth. Americans saw world government conspiracies everywhere they looked. They viewed the United Nations, the

International Court of Justice and any sort of international agreement as a step towards world government. They talked about the Illuminata and endless theories about world government ruled by the devil. Many Americans opposed international agreements banning the use of land mines, reducing the amount of hydro carbons pumped into the air or any other international agreement on any subject. Jamie viewed himself as an internationalist. He disliked the expression "God Bless America" not because he didn't love his country. He did love his country but thought it vulgar to ask a God, any God, to bless just one country. He wasn't convinced that there was a God but if there was he thought any God would be angered if asked to bless just one country. If Jamie were going to ask God to issue a blessing it would have been to Bless the World. Jamie also believed that the wealth of the world was unevenly distributed and he thought that the world would be a better place if wealth were more evenly distributed. It seemed evil to him that so many of the world's people went hungry while so many others were fat and able to waste food. So in principal, Jamie would have welcomed a World government and a more equitable distribution of wealth even though this might mean that his wealth would part of that re-distributed.

In England lived a man who wanted to help create a World government. This man came from a family background which had bestowed upon him the title of Lord. He was not an idle member of the British favored class. He was an international banker and it was his role as a banker which had brought him to Jamie's attention. After years of tracing the flow of money from the Saudis to those who were carrying out attacks on the United States Jamie had traced the control of this money to this British banker. He had done so with the use of software programs which keyed him into correspondence which used certain key words. In this case the key word which attracted his attention was WTC which he knew stood for World Trade

Center. In much of the correspondence he reviewed the

reference to WTC was innocent but his program went a step

further and pointed him to all correspondence with WTC and

references to airliners. The program led him to a power point

presentation which had been created by a London banker.

The banker was a member of a British family and the Banker

was a Lord in a long line of Lords who had controlled

Britain's largest bank for three generations.

 Many Europeans considered Americans "outlaws" because

the American government had consistently refused to take

part in many of the international protocols which Europeans

thought would make the world a better and safer place to

live. This feeling was particularly strong among the British

supporters of the creation of a World government. Many of

the British viewed the United States as the single greatest

obstacle to a stable world government. They viewed

American wealth and power

as something which had to be curtailed if they were to be permitted to create what they thought would be a better world, ruled by a world government. This banker, this Lord, believed that the United States would have to be destroyed as a world power so that he and his world government believers could prevail. His family's involvement in Arabia went back to the days of the legendary T.E. Lawrence- *"Lawrence of Arabia"*.

In his book "The Seven Pillars of Wisdom" Lawrence said:

" *All men dream, but not equally. Those who dream by night in the dusty recesses of their minds wake in the day to find that it was vanity: but the dreamers of the day are dangerous men, for they may act their dreams with open eyes, to make it possible*"

The Lord was one of those who sought to make a dream reality. He was a dangerous man. Through T.E. Lawrence, who was revered by the Sheikhs of Arabia and, ultimately by the founder of Saudi Arabia,

King bin Saud, the Lord's grandfather had become King bin Saud's banker after oil was discovered in the kingdom in 1938. The Lord was the third generation of his family to serve the House of Saud. The Lord had even persuaded the House of Saud that he was a convert to the narrow version of Islam supported by the House of Saud. Of course the Lord also attended his local Church of England each Sunday and professed to be a Christian. Like many of the members of the House of Saud the Lord had a dual existence. He was both British and Saudi, Muslem and Christian. What ever suited his purpose or helped him pursue his dream of a world government.

For much of the first part of the 20th Century Britain was a power in the Middle East. As countries like Syria, Eqypt, Iran, Iraq and Lebanon developed secular leaders who tried to gain independence for their countries the British sought to bolster fundamentalist Islamic movements throughout the Middle East so they could continue to control the Middle East. It was the British who financed and supported the Muslim Brotherhood using Islam as a rallying call. All through the 20th Century it was to the advantage of the British to support the Saudi's support for fundamental Islam throughout the Kingdom. The House of Sauds' long ancestral connection with Wahhabism allowed the kingdom to use Islam as a rallying point so they could maintain control of Saudi Arabia. As the 20th Century was ending a larger and larger rift between the U.S. and Europeans who supported one world government developed. It seemed to many of the British that the U.S. sought to limit or reduce the power of the United Nations. Historically Americans had always opposed giving up national power in favor of international power. The United States opposed most of the international agreements Europeans thought were useful in making the world a better place to live. It seemed to many Europeans that the United States was a rogue nation. It seemed clear to the Lord that the creation of a world government would only come about with a weakened United States. It was natural for the Lord and others that thought like him to continue to tell the Saudis that they needed to attack the U.S. in defense of Islam. The Lord knew that he could not directly advocate an attack on the U.S. Britain was still closely allied with the U.S. so the Lord put together a sophisticated plan whereby commercial airliners loaded with jet fuel would be hijacked and crashed into strategic targets in the U.S. The Lord needed to make sure that the plans he developed could not be traced back to him. He also wanted to try to make sure that the plans couldn't be traced to the House of Saud. The solution was to find a stalking horse. His name was Osama bin Laden. First the Lord put into the minds of key members of the House of Saud that they needed to create a "stalking horse" to do their deeds without those deeds being connected to the House of Saud. For many years the House of bin Laden had served the House of Saud and as a member of the House of bin Laden Osama bin Laden agreed to serve in this battle. He was told by his mentors in the House of Saud that the world would need to believe that Osama and the House of Saud were enemies. If the U.S. perceived that the House of Saud was directing the actions of Osama bin Laden the House of Saud would lose its' best customer and would probably face the wrath of the U.S. military. For many years the House of Saud financed religious schools in Afghanistan which taught the strict Islamic views of the Wahhabist. This led to the creation of the Taliban which by 2001 ruled most of the fractured, divided country of Afghanistan. In fact it had been many years since any central government had ruled all or most of Afghanistan. In fact Afghanistan was ruled by a collection of regional war lords. With the support of the Taliban Osama bin Laden set up training camps to prepare an army for attacks on the United States both in the United States and on US interests worldwide.

The Lord was born in a nursery in the ancestral home his family had lived in for more than 200 years. His mother was attended by the family doctor and a mid-wife. His early education had been at a boarding school in Scotland to which his father and grandfather had also been sent when they were boys. He matriculated to Trinity College at Cambridge where he was a good student. His education prepared him to follow the profession of his father and grandfather. They were bankers. After finishing at Cambridge he was sent to work in the Geneva branch of the bank his father headed. It was one of the largest banks in the world with branches in nearly every capitol of every country in the world. Like his father he took an early interest in world affairs as he watched the British Empire dwindle in size and influence. He had been born during the war but the family estate was far enough from London to avoid the bombs rained down on the city by the Germans. After five years working at the Geneva branch of the bank his father ran, he was transferred to Paris where he worked for five more years. His next posting was to Egypt where he ran the Cairo branch of the bank. Next he spent five years in Riyadh where he came to know the most powerful members of the Royal Family. He spoke flawless Arabic and knew as much about the Wahhabi strain of Islam as most Clerics. He also became very friendly with the bin Laden family and was an intimate of Osama bin Laden. He enjoyed playing basketball with the lanky Osama. Osama, although tall, was flat footed and not a very good player. After five years in Riyadh, upon his father's death, he returned to England and became the President of the bank which his family had controlled for more than sixty years. He had married a Swiss woman during his years in Geneva and she had given him two sons and a daughter. His wife and daughter had been killed in a car accident during the time he was working in Egypt and he had never re-married. He spent all of his waking hours on bank business or on work devoted to the organization of which he was a member. The organization sought to promote the establishment of a world government. However, the Lord maintained a low profile in his work for a world government. Although he was one of the most powerful men in the world he kept a low profile and studiously avoided the limelight. His one favorite pastime was fox hunting. He liked to ride in the hunt and loved the sounds of the hunt. The dogs baying, the horns sounding, the sounds of the horses and riders. He understood that he was part of a privileged class. His only major vice was that he had a large collection of child pornography. Twice a year he would vacation in Thailand where he would arrange to spend the night with a young girl. He liked girls of 10 or 11. They had to be virgins. He could afford the best. He also liked to take photos of the young girls. During the visits to Thailand he would also hire a young girl, 11 was a good age, and bring in a man with a large penis who he would photograph raping the young girl. This always excited him. He was a world traveler as at home in London as in New York City. Although he belonged to several international organizations he remained in the background of each of them.

Chapter 12- Martin Luther King and a Bitter Strike

After quitting his job with the Army Jamie flew to Memphis to be with Donna and Cindy. Donna, in her ninth month of pregnancy, looked absolutely radiant. The impending birth had swollen her breasts and her nipples looked like prunes. Cindy was really looking forward to the new baby. She didn't know if she would have a baby sister or a baby brother but she didn't care. A short time after Jamie arrived back in Memphis Donna had a baby boy. The delivery had come with no complications. Donna had awakened Jamie at 2 a.m. and he had driven her to the hospital. Twenty minutes after they arrived at the hospital the baby was born. They named him James Reece after Jamie's grandfather , J.R. During the next few weeks Jamie talked with Donna about what they should do next. After resigning from the Army he was a "hot" property. As one of McNamara's "Quiz" kids many employers wanted him to come to work. He was particularly sought after by defense contractors. However, he had vowed not to work on any job that directly supported the war. During his time back in Memphis his views had solidified and he had become fervently opposed to the War. He had joined a group known as the Vietnam Veterans Against the War and he had gone back to D.C. to take part in mass protests. In one protest in what was called the Mobilization Against the War he had taken part in what was called the March against Death. Marchers assembled near the Arlington National Cemetery. Every few seconds a Marcher with a sign bearing the name of someone killed in Vietnam and carrying a candle would leave to march across the bridge into the District past the Lincoln Memorial and along Pennsylvania Avenue past the White House. It was a cold, windy, rainy day and many of the Marchers had trouble keeping their candles lit. As a marcher reached the White House they would blow out their candles. Some threw the candle onto the White House lawn. Some veterans threw their medals onto the lawn. When Jamie reached the White House he blew out his candle and threw the medal that the South Vietnamese had given him for saving the life of the crane operator during the helicopter crash which had broken his collar bone over the white house fence.

While he was in D.C. he had lunch with Robert McNamara who was nearing the end of his time as Secretary of Defense. McNamara was beginning to have second thoughts about Vietnam but was not yet ready to admit that he had been wrong. Jamie told McNamara of his own feelings and McNamara praised him for making up his mind and acting upon his beliefs. After a few weeks to think it over Jamie accepted a job in Memphis with the Internal Revenue Service. The job permitted him to live in Memphis which allowed both he and Donna to be near their parents. It also permitted him to return to school to continue his education. The IRS hired Jamie as a Revenue Officer at a GS level 9. As a Revenue Officer it was his job to collect tax revenue and seek compliance with the IRS Code. After he was hired the IRS send Jamie to Miami Beach to be trained. The group of new Revenue Officers was a spirited bunch. They were mostly young men and several, like Jamie, had served in Vietnam. There were some real characters in the group. When they weren't attending classes many in the group went chasing women and drinking in the bars and night clubs of Miami Beach. However, Jamie had brought Donna, Cindy and J.R. with him and so when the day's classes were done he always went straight back to his motel. While Jamie was in class each day, Donna would sunbath on the beach with the kids and had gotten a beautiful tan which made her body glow with good health. Most of the other Revenue Officers had left their wives or girlfriends home and upon seeing Donna, they all envied Jamie. They all admired the way Donna looked in a bathing suit. Her body was trim and showed no signs that she was the mother of two children. Jamie was kidded unmercifully because he never went out with the others when they went into the Miami night looking for women. They called their hunt "Poon Tang Time". They liked to call Jamie pussy whipped but secretly they could understand why he preferred to spend his evenings with Donna and the kids.

Jamie was a standout in the group of thirty Revenue Officers being trained. He was a natural born leader and the other men looked to him for leadership. Towards the end of the three weeks of training Jamie was approached by a Revenue Agent who worked in the Miami area. The agent headed a task force which was investigating organized crime in that area. Most of the big hotels in Miami Beach were owned by organized crime families.

The agent asked Jamie if he would stay in Miami after the classes ended and accept a six week assignment working with the task force. Jamie talked it over with Donna and she agreed that staying in Miami Beach another six weeks would be nice.

The task force gave Jamie a new identity and the academic credentials of an accountant and he was instructed to get a job with a Miami based trucking company which the IRS believed was owned by an organized crime family. The trucking company looked just like any other trucking company. No swarthy Italians staggered around the premises. When he went to apply for the job at the company as an accountant he was greeted at the front office by a receptionist who gave him an application to complete. Even though it was a hot day Jamie was dressed in a dark blue suit, long sleeved white dress shirt and a conservative tie. His shoes were freshly polished and he was calm and collected as he completed the application and was interviewed by the Accounting Manager. His new name was John Doyle and his application indicated that he had graduated from the University of Illinois with a degree in Accounting. The Accounting Manager was an attractive middle aged blond woman, Joanne, who liked what she saw as she interviewed Jamie. She flirted with Jamie all the way through the interview. After the interview she asked Jamie to wait a few minutes so he could be interviewed by the General Manager. In a few minutes he was escorted into the General Manager's office whose name was Albert. He was about 5-10, with receding blond hair and blue eyes. He had a powerful looking body and looked as if he may have once driven a truck. After introducing himself to Jamie they made small talk for a few minutes. The chemistry between the two men was good. Jamie liked the way Albert presented himself. Jamie regretted why he was there. He felt sneaky and dishonest. He knew he was going to get the job and he did. He started work the following Monday. His job was simple. He prepared payrolls and produced weekly and monthly reports reflecting the income and expenses of the company. His job for the IRS wasn't quite so easy. He was directed to determine where the income from the company actually went. The company was a Delaware corporation and that corporation was owned by two other Delaware corporations which were, in turn owned by a corporation based in the Bahamas. The Bahamian corporation was owned by a trust company. All the drivers who worked for the company belonged to the Teamsters but the company never had labor union problems. The company had been accused of using "strong arm" tactics to get trucking contracts but Jamie saw no strong arms hanging around the office. Several of the company's competitors had suffered unexplained labor union difficulties but no one had connected it to this company. Jamie fit in quickly at the company. He got along well with everyone. The office staff, of which Jamie was a part, consisted of ten people. In addition the company employed a traffic manager, a contract manager, a scheduler / router and more than 300 truck drivers. Jamie joined the office softball team and during the first game got three hits including a game winning homerun. He was also the winning pitcher. Jamie liked the people he worked with and he felt like a real creep. It wasn't easy for him to live a lie. He was also frustrated by how little information he was able to pass on to his IRS supervisor. Finding out where the company's money went was an impossible task. He was only able to provide part of what was a giant jig saw puzzle. Their were no unusual expenses reflected on expense ledgers and if any money was being siphoned off to organized crime it was well concealed. After five, unproductive weeks with the company the IRS had Jamie resign from the job and return to Memphis. His job as an "undercover" agent was over. It had all been so low key. No excitement. No one getting shot or stabbed. The IRS task force of more than 250 agents was investigating 88 businesses in Miami Beach. Not all of the undercover operatives were as fortunate as Jamie. The body of one Agent was found floating in Biscayne Bay. Someone had taken him fishing and had used him as bait to troll for sharks.

Jamie, Donna and their children returned to Memphis in the Fall. During the day Jamie worked for the IRS and at night he took college classes. Vietnam continued to knaw at Jamie. The news reports from Vietnam were hard to ignore as the casualties continued to mount. By this time Jamie was bitterly opposed to the war and he found it difficult in polite conversations to hide his bitter thoughts. Few of his co-workers knew that Jamie had served in Vietnam. He never talked about it. However, at the college he was attending Jamie began attending meetings of a student group, Students for a Democratic Society (SDS), which was strongly against the war in Vietnam. He never said anything at the meetings. He only sat and listened. He knew that the meetings were attended by undercover agents from many different organizations. Army Intelligence, Navy Intelligence, the FBI, the Tennessee Bureau of Intelligence, the Memphis City Police, the Shelby County Sheriff's Department. He could generally spot undercover agents by the way that they dressed and the type shoes they wore. At some meetings he thought that as many as one fourth of those in attendance were undercover agents spying on the group. Many of the students assumed that Jamie was an undercover agent. He was always dressed in a dark suit, white dress shirt and conservative tie. He was clean shaven and always kept his hair neatly trimmed. Many of the students had long hair and beards and many dressed as if they had bought all their clothing at an Army Surplus store. The grunge look was in and many of the students smelled of marijuana. S.D.S. was a loose knit organization and no one actually belonged to the organization. There were no membership dues and no lists of members. Those who were regular attendees at meeting, other than the undercover agents, had a range of political views ranging from conservative to avowed members of the American Communist Party. Some belonged to organizations dedicated to obscure figures of the early 20th century left. The Rosa Luxembourg society was particularly popular with many of the women. Their was also a group dedicated to the ill fated Leon Trotsky, who had been chased down in Mexico and executed by the Russians after he had competed with Joseph Stalin for power in post 1917 Russia. Regardless of the view of those who regularly attended SDS they all had one thing in common. They could rarely agree on anything and they were all under surveillance by at least one agency. The underground agents who attended all of the SDS meetings also assumed that Jamie was one of them. In listening to the various SDS leaders Jamie concluded that they were a pretty harmless and light weight group. Most were college students in the late teens or early 20's and had really very little understanding of what the Vietnam War was really about. Jamie sat quietly at all of the meetings and took no part in the discussions. This all changed on a Friday afternoon on a cool December day a few days before the new year. SDS had scheduled a demonstration opposing the war to be held in front of the federal building where Jamie worked. The demonstration was centered around a flat bed truck with a speaker platform and a loud speaker. It had just started as Jamie was scheduled to leave work for the day. He had a choice. He could go out a side door and go home to Donna or he could go out the front door where the demonstration was being held. He walked out the front door. The crowd of curious people and SDS supporters numbered about 150. Several television news teams from local stations were photographing the proceedings. Some of the demonstrators were carrying signs and chanting anti war slogans. "Hey, Hey LBJ how many kids did you kill today." "Stop the War" and other slogans which were common in the Anti Vietnam War movement. The local leader of the SDS, Walter, a tall, thin 21 year old, who was in one of Jamie's classes was trying to make a speech. The kid, as Jamie thought of him, had great difficulty in keeping the crowd focused on what he was saying and he was looking for a way to end his speech. Walter saw Jamie walking along the outside fringes of the crowd and he yelled to Jamie to come forward and say a few words. Walter thought Jamie was an undercover agent and he thought this might be a good way to embarrass him. As Walter gestured towards Jamie the camera crews swung their cameras toward him. For a moment Jamie hesitated and than he walked up the steps to the microphone. The crowd was grateful at the prospect of hearing someone other than Walter but Jamie didn't look like what they expected. Walter had a wispy beard and long hair and was dressed like a refuge from a combat zone. Jamie was wearing a dark suit, white dress shirt and conservative tie which is what he would normally wear for his IRS job. He had a briefcase under one arm along with his folded overcoat. He felt a chill as the cameras focused on him and the crowd waited for him to say something. Jamie knew he should mumble a few trite phrases and get back away from the microphone before he attracted too much attention. If he didn't say anything newsworthy he knew the reporters wouldn't say anything about him on the evening news. He didn't want to say anything that would get him on the evening news. But in the back of his mind he remembered the body bags he had ridden with in Vietnam. He knew that the young men in those bags were silent forever. What would they say if they could speak, wondered Jamie. But they couldn't speak. They lie in graves all over the country in small towns and big cities. Jamie began to speak slowly about what he had seen in Vietnam. He spoke from the heart without trying to get across a particular point. He lost himself in what he was saying. He told the crowd he wanted to tell them what he had seen in Vietnam. The crowd got very quiet as Jamie described what he had seen. His words were cutting and bitter. Those who had only been half listening were now listening intently to what he said. He told them about the young soldier he had watched die. He said the soldier was a handsome young man with a thatch of blond hair and a beautifully formed muscular young body. On his uniform he wore the insignia of a Second Lt. His uniform and body were unmarked except for a small hole in his chest through which his life was ebbing away. He told the crowd what it was like to watch this young man bleed and die and he asked "what did this man die for". "For whom did he die" He told the crowd about the Vietnamese businessman and this man's three adult children who were far from the war going to school in France. He told them about the prosperity he had seen around defense plants in Connecticut. He told them about Ho Chi Minh who he described as Vietnam's

George Washington. He told the crowd about the pile of bodies he had seen being tallied for a body count. Among the bodies being counted were those of several small children. He remembered one body in particular. It was the body of a pretty little Vietnamese girl about age six who was wearing a parochial school uniform with a pink ribbon in her black hair. Her body was already stiff from death and had a waxen look but she was still a pretty little girl even in death. Her hand lie at her side and in her hand was the hand of a boy who looked as if he might have been her older brother. The crowd was silent as Jamie asked "Why did they die". What sort of war and what sort of country killed little girls wearing pink ribbons in their hair? What sort of country would count these children as part of a body count to show how well the war was going? What sort of people would throw this little dead girl into a big hole in the ground and cover her with dirt. Jamie provided the answer. Only an evil country in an evil war and he concluded by saying that anyone who supported this war was either ignorant or evil. With that Jamie left the platform and walked away before any of the reporters could talk with him. It was an emotional and bitter speech and it was shown on all of the local news broadcasts that evening. Jamie had made no political statements other than to say the war was evil. All of the undercover agents had noted what Jamie had said and several were moved and shaken by what he had said. They knew that Jamie was something new to the antiwar movement in Memphis. He was obviously the real deal to be taken seriously. Jamie had only told the crowd what he had seen and what he had come to believe. Jamie's phone was ringing when he got home. Donna had answered some of the first calls but after fielding some obscene callers was now letting the phone ring. Many of the callers called Jamie names and questioned his patriotism. This, of course, made Jamie very angry. He thought the war was bad for America and he thought it was patriotic to say so. He thought he had the right to freely express himself. After all wasn't the war about "freedom"? His phone continued to ring all weekend and newspaper reporters came to his house for interviews. He turned them all away. Jamie was still badly stung and angry when he returned to work the following Monday. There were 20 Revenue Officers in Jamie's group and they were a pretty close knit group. Jamie was well liked by the group. Every one of them had seen Jamie's speech on the news over the weekend. It had been replayed many times by the local stations. All of his fellow Revenue Officers accepted what Jamie had said as true and several told him it had changed how they thought about the war. Every one of them came by to Jamie that morning to tell him "way to go". During the morning coffee break all of the Revenue Officers sat around a table quietly until one said "Wow Jamie you really laid it on".

Later that morning Jamie was called into the office of his supervisor. His supervisor was a quiet man nearing retirement at age 60. He had served in combat in the Pacific during World War which had left him with a deep hatred for all wars. He was scheduled to retire in a few months and was looking forward to being able to spend more time fishing at his favorite lake. He politely directed Jamie to a seat across the desk from him. He told Jamie that his speech had attracted lots of attention. The District Director of the IRS had called from Nashville to say that he had received calls from Members of Congress, the FBI and the Memphis Police Department wanting to know if Jamie really did work for the IRS. He told Jamie "A lot of people want your hide". He went on to say. "Jamie, I agree with everything you said but as you know the federal law known as the Hatch Act prohibits federal employees from taking part in a political campaign". Both men were silent for a moment. "I told the District Director that you weren't involved in a political campaign and I told him yes you were one of my employees and that I was proud of you". "But for both of our goods please- be careful".

During the rest of the week Jamie did his best to avoid additional publicity. He didn't attend SDS meetings even though many of the kids in SDS now were seeking him out for conversations. He was asked to appear on a local TV program to discuss the Vietnam War but he declined to appear. He also declined requests for interview from local reporters. His speech had been picked up by the national news media and had appeared on all the networks. He had to change his telephone number. Teachers at Cindy's school had told her that her father was a "commie". This really made Jamie angry and he vowed to take Cindy out of school when school resumed after the New Year's holiday. It was New Year's Eve and Jamie had begun to hope the furor would die down. Because it would be a short work day for Jamie and his co-workers everyone was in a good mood. The other Revenue Officers had erected a protective "net" around Jamie. They all belonged to the National Association of Internal Revenue Employees and they believed that Jamie had the right to say what he had said. The local representative of the Union had issued a statement defending Jamie. During lunch one of Jamie's coworkers rushed up to him waiving the front page of the local afternoon newspaper. Jamie's photo was on the front page next to a photo of J. Edgar Hoover, the cross dresser, who was the head of the F.B.I. Below the photos was an article by Hoover saying that SDS was a communist front organization. Next to the article by Hoover was a local side bar article describing Jamie as the "leader" of the local SDS chapter and saying that he was a full time employee of the IRS and a student at the local university. Jamie was glad it was to be a short workday but he also knew that now the shit was really going to hit the fan.

1968 was a pivotal year in U.S. history and it was a pivotal year in Jamie's life. Even though the Memphis media had labeled him the leader of the SDS most of the SDS members considered him an outsider. The IRS had sent him a warning letter telling him to comply with the provisions of the Hatch Act. The Hatch Act prohibited federal employees from taking part in a political campaign. Jamie was not taking part in a political campaign. Jamie was receiving daily threats both by mail and by phone. One threat in particular alarmed Jamie. A caller had threatened to firebomb Jamie's house that night. One of Jamie's friends, a tough former Green Beret who had served two tours in Vietnam, sat on the roof of Jamie's house that night with an M-1 Carbine waiting for anyone to try to firebomb Jamie's house. Jamie had not filed a complaint with the police since he believed that many of the threats were coming from the police. It was a tense night for Jamie. He was afraid his friend might shoot the paperboy when he came by early next morning to deliver the morning newspaper. Donna and the children had moved in with her parents so that if anything did happen they would be safe.

At the university he was attending at nights many of the other students were treating Jamie like a hero. He was approached by the President of the schools Black Student Association and asked to speak to a meeting of the Black Student Association. In 1968 the school was about 15% black and several of the black students were Vietnam Vets. They had seen Jamie's speech on TV and they wanted to hear him at one of their meetings. The invitation to Jamie was controversial within the group. This was the time in history when many black students were anti-white and into what they called "Black Power". Many of them didn't want a white man to speak before the group. Several black veterans in the group had pushed to have Jamie speak because they hoped he could articulate their own experiences in the war. When

Jamie appeared to speak at the meeting he could tell that some of the 100 or so people attending were hostile to him. Before he could be introduced a young man in the audience wearing a colorful dashiki rose to question the President of the BSA who had invited Jamie to the meeting. The young man said "Why is this Honkie here?" "We don't need no white man to tell us about Vietnam". "We got plenty of brothers dying there already" The BSA President was at a loss for words and so he said that he would have Jamie answer that question. "By what measure am I white" said Jamie. "My maternal grandmother was a full blooded Cherokee and by most definitions concerning race that makes me "colored". At this the young man sat down and the crowd cheered. Jamie went on to describe the recent history of Vietnam and to suggest that all the Vietnamese were trying to do was gain their independence. He also talked about the role race played in Vietnam. The toughest and most dangerous jobs in Vietnam went to black men. Combat units were disproportionately black. Most officers were white. Fewer blacks could go to college and therefore fewer got deferments from the draft. He also talked about the racial terms that many in the U.S. military used in describing the Vietnamese. He said that the word "Gook" was just like a certain "N" word used by many racists in Memphis to describe black people. By the time he had finished speaking many in the crowd were nodding their heads in agreement with Jamie. When he finished speaking the crowd, including the young man in the dashiki, stood and applauded. Many came to shake his hand afterwards. One large black man rose from one of the seats and came towards Jamie with a large grin. When Jamie saw who it was his face broke into an ear to ear smile. The two men exchanged a enthusiastic bear hug. It was Billy Tyler home from the Jungle. He had just returned to Memphis after 13 months in Da Nang with the Marines. Billy and Jamie had first met 15 years before at the "colored" playground near the first place his family had lived when they first came to Memphis. Over the years Jamie and Billy had become close friends. After they hugged and patted each other on the back Billy moved to the microphone and told the crowd how he and Jamie had first met and how they had become close friends over the years. He told the crowd "This man is a brother regardless of how pale his skin is" The BSA President took the microphone and asked the crowd if Jamie should be made an honorary member. The crowd, including the young man in the dashiki, roared their consent and approval. His role as an honorary member of the BSA quickly became much more than Jamie had expected. In February of 1968 something happened in Memphis which set in motion events leading to a great tragedy. The garbage men in the City of Memphis were city employees and almost all of them were black. In Memphis whites didn't become garbage men. The garbage men in Memphis were members of the American Federation of State, County and Municipal Employees of the American Federation of Labor. They worked under terrible and dangerous conditions. The City of Memphis called them sanitation workers but the conditions under which they worked were anything but sanitary. During a work day which began before dawn they were given lunch breaks of 15 minutes and infrequent bathroom breaks. They brought their lunches to work in brown bags and lunch buckets but when it was lunch time they had no place to wash their hands. The job was dirty and dangerous. They rode on the back of garbage trucks and several had been killed when caught by the compression mechanism of the big trucks which was designed to crush the garbage which they collected. The families of those who were killed received only a small stipend upon the death of their loved one. All of the drivers of the big trucks were white and all of the supervisors were white. The working conditions of the drivers and supervisors weren't much better than that of the garbage collectors but at least they could look down upon the blacks who picked up the heavy garbage cans and thrust their contents into the yawl of the big trucks. The strike began after another black man was crushed to death when the crushing mechanism on a truck malfunctioned. When the strike began no one thought it would last very long. Most of the garbage men had families to feed and no savings which they could use to tide them over. A few days after the strike the Mayor of Memphis declared that if the men didn't return to work he would fire them all and begin hiring replacements. The militancy of the Mayor escalated what had begun as a labor union issue into a civil rights issue. In his statement the Mayor had asked the "boys" to return to work. It was not uncommon in the American South for white people to refer to adult blacks as "boy" or "girl" but this time it hit a nerve in the black community. Many of the black churches in Memphis began supporting the strikers and helping to feed their families. One black minister, originally from Detroit, called a friend in Atlanta and asked for his support for the strike. This friend in Atlanta was no ordinary man. He was also a minister but he also led a civil rights group known as the Southern Christian Leadership Conference. The man was the Reverend Dr. Martin Luther King, a Nobel Peace Prize Laureate. The Black Student Association was asked to help organize students in support of the strikers. The BSA , in turn, asked Jamie to organize white students in support of the strike. Although this was not an easy job Jamie quickly put together a large group of white students to support the strikers. Many whites, even in Memphis, felt sympathy for the strikers because this strike was not just black vs. white. It was poor vs. rich and labor vs. management and almost everyone likes an underdog. Jamie quickly became a pivotal figure in the strike because of his ability to turn out hundreds of whites in support of the strikers. Most of these were college students but he also found a lot of ordinary whites who supported the strikers. In his core group of white supporters of the strike were many nuns and priests and a few ministers from local churches. Any white minister from a local church risked being fired if his congregation found about his support for the strike. A number of white housewives, many who had moved to Memphis from other areas of the country also came out to support the strikers and helped raise money to support the families of the strikers. At one demonstration that Jamie organized more than 2000 people turned out. About 50 counter demonstrators left when they saw the size of the crowd. The store window of the local John Birch Society's bookstore had a list of people that they labeled the most subversive in Memphis. Jamie's name was number two on the list.

When the SCLC sent its leaders to Memphis Jamie was invited to sit in on the meetings. He also arranged for Dr. King to speak on campus but shortly before he was scheduled to speak the school withdrew permission to use the school's auditorium and Dr. King's group was turned away at the entrance to the campus. The group needed a place to meet to discuss finding a new place to speak and so Jamie suggested they all go to his house near the campus. The group, in five black Cadillac's loaned to them by a local funeral home, drove to Jamie's house. Donna looked through the front window and was shocked by what she saw. The kids were at school. Up the sidewalk came Jamie and a large group of black people. On the street were parked the black Cadillac's followed by several vans of TV crews. As always the house was in perfect order and during the meeting Donna was the perfect hostess serving, coffee, tea and lemonade. She had also made cookies earlier in the day and these were passed around and were soon gone. The group's meeting lasted an hour until a local church, near the campus, agreed that Dr. King could speak in the churches auditorium. It was all quite an experience for Donna. After all she was a "Southern Belle" and her family was from Mississippi, and here was Martin Luther King, one of the most respected, loved and hated men in the world sitting in her living room. Dr. King and his staff lavished praise on Donna saying politely thank you for the beverages and for the cookies.

The SCLC decided they would hold a march in downtown Memphis in support of the strike. They issued invitations for people to come from all over the world. They wanted to make sure the march was peaceful. One problem quickly arose. Many young blacks were turned off by the non violent approach of Dr. King and the SCLC. Many of them were members of a local militant group known as the Invaders. The Invaders were openly anti-white and preached that things should be changed through violence. The leader of the Invaders was a charismatic young man with whom Jamie had played basketball fifteen years earlier. He was also a close friend of Billy Tyler but now Billy thought his friend was a little bit crazy. The leader of the Invaders was known as "Sweet Willie Wine" and even though he was fervently anti white he and Jamie continued to be friends. Sweet Willie often said Jamie was his only remaining white friend. A few months earlier the mostly racist Memphis police had thrown Sweet Willie in jail. He wasn't charged with a crime but was told he would stay in jail until he posted a $50,000. "Peace Bond" to guarantee he wouldn't commit a crime. Sweet Willie didn't have the money. Jamie thought that what the City of Memphis was trying to do, to shut Sweet Willie up, was outrageous so he went to a very wealthy elderly Jewish leader who was the father of one of Jamie's friends from his first school days in Memphis and this man agreed that he would post this peace bond. The only thing he required was that no one be told who had put up the money. After his release Jamie picked Sweet Willie up at the jail to take him home. Sweet Willie, and several hundred of his supporters, lived in a poor area of North Memphis. Their group had taken over a square city block of what were known as "Shotgun Houses". A shotgun house was a house which, with the front and back doors opened, nothing would be touched if someone fired a shotgun through the front door. The Invaders had set up lookouts to warn them when the police were in the neighborhood. They had built tunnels which allowed them to go from house to house without being seen. When Sweet Willie got to the Shotgun House which was his home he invited Jamie in. Jamie was amazed by what he saw. From the outside the house looked as if it might collapse at any time. Inside the house was neat and clean and well furnished. Sweet Willie took Jamie through the tunnels under the houses and showed him an underground area contained hundreds of weapons. It was very scary.

As the SCLC began to plan the March they tried to make peace with the Invaders.

However, the Invaders wanted to participate in the March with their own section and with their own signs. The SCLC would not agree to this. The SCLC also would not agree to let any of the Invaders serve as Marshals for the parade. On the day of the March thousands of people gathered at a large church, Claiborne Temple, just off the main street of the black community, Beale Street. The March was to proceed West on Beale to Main Street, which was where the largely white business district began, and North on Main to the Federal Building. The planners of the March were amazed at the number of people who came for the March. Contingents had flown in from all over the United States and from many foreign countries. Messages of support had poured in from union and political leaders from all over the world. It was a festive atmosphere and the Marchers were all in a good mood. Martin Luther King and several dignitaries were to be at the Head of the March. Jamie was at the head of more than a thousand whites and had brought his daughter Cindy with him to ride on his shoulders. However, right before the March was to begin Sweet Willie came by and told Jamie not to take Cindy with him during the March. Instead Jamie left her with the friendly women who were running a day care center in the Church for children of the Marchers. Donna had remained at home with J.R. Many of the Marchers carried signs which said simply "I am a Man". The March began peacefully. The Memphis City Police gave the Marchers plenty of room. The front of the March made the turn and began to proceed down Main Street. After about a fourth of the Marchers had made the turn onto Main Street to proceed past a large downtown department store a large group of Invaders who were carrying signs which said "I am a Man" tore the signs off the wooden sticks on which the signs had been stapled and rushed to the sidewalks and began breaking department store windows on Main Street. This was just what the Memphis police were waiting for and they stopped the March and began lobbing tear gas canisters into the largely peaceful crowd. Most of the Memphis cops were too slow to run and catch the young members of the Invaders who were breaking windows so they did what they really wanted to do. They stopped the March and began clubbing everyone in sight.. The large crowd seeing the clouds of tear gas and hearing the sounds of police sirens and police whistles began to panic and a stampede ensued. Many of the elderly Marchers were knocked to the ground and run over by Marchers trying to flee. When the panic began Jamie ducked safely into a store on Beale Street where he knew the owner. The March turned into a disaster. The SCLC was accused of planning the destruction of property. In fact most of the property destruction was caused by the police. Only a few windows were broken by the Invaders. Most windows were broken by the police pushing people through windows or by teargas canisters thrown by the police. By the time Jamie got back to Claiborne

Temple to pick up Cindy the large church was being used to treat the hundreds of people who had been injured. The March gave the SCLC a black eye

And many white Memphians began calling Martin Luther King "Marching Looter King". The SCLC was angry at the Invaders and angry at themselves for not having enough marshals to control the Marchers. It was a victory for the Invaders but a black eye for the strikers many of whom had sons who belonged to the Invaders. Many of the whites who opposed the strike thought they had won a victory that day but they simply didn't understand the significance of what had actually happened. The news of the March which the police had turned into chaos and the tear gas and the beatings administered by police went all over the world. The police violence was condemned in London, Paris, Amsterdam, Oslo, Copenhagen and many other places. The only country which said anything in support of the City of Memphis and its police department was South

Africa. Nelson Mandela was still in a South African prison and the reaction of the white South African government was not surprising. The sanitation strike in Memphis, which had begun as a low key local labor issue, was now a full blown international cause celebre. Media people from all over the world poured into Memphis. It was a classic struggle. The white leadership of Memphis was confident of victory. They continued to say they were going to fire all the garbage men and hire new ones. The garbage continued to pile up and the foreign media saw an ugly Memphis. The Memphis leadership was composed of fools. The handwriting was on the wall in letters a hundred feet tall and they couldn't read it. More than anything the struggle had boiled down to good vs. evil and Memphis had weighed in on the side of evil. They sought to defend the practices of the past, the discrimination, the fearful working conditions, the subsistence wages, the denial of opportunity. Much of the world outside the white South saw the Memphis leaders as villains. Even LBJ, in control of the federal government, knew that the Memphis leaders were fighting a losing battle. But Henry Loeb, the pugnacious, ignorant Mayor of Memphis, thought he was going to win. He thought he could stand in the doorway of history and block its' overpowering strength.

As the furor from the March began to subside the SCLC began plans for the next March. It was necessary to have a second March to prove that they could have a peaceful March. The City of Memphis immediately issued an Order prohibiting a second March. The SCLC was forced to go into federal court to seek an injunction ordering the City of Memphis to honor the Bill of Rights and allow the March to go forward. The outcome was inevitable but history was moving to a bitter climax. The strike was deadlocked. Mayor Loeb and the City of Memphis continued to take a hard line but they had been unable to hire replacements for the garbage men. The garbage continued to pile up and Memphis continued to get the sort of worldwide bad publicity that no city wants to receive. Mayor Loeb found it impossible to yield even if he had been smart enough to do so. And he wasn't. If he yielded the white voters who had elected him Mayor would have made him a political pariah. Feelings were running high. Nearly every member of the black community supported the strikers although they were careful not to admit to their white employers how they felt. Most of the white community with the exception of a few "liberals" and a few "out of towners" supported Mayor Loeb. Many of the white students who supported the strikers were from areas outside the South. From Illinois, Ohio, New York, California and other areas of the country. It looked as if the strike would go on forever. The City of Memphis which had prided itself on being the "Cleanest City in America" was starting to look and smell very bad. It was not just that the garbage was piling up. The image of the city was taking a terrible beating all over the world. Stories about the dirty and dangerous working conditions and the subsistence wages under which the cities garbage men were forced to work were appearing all over the world. Memphis was swarming with foreign reporters and the stories they send back to their countries rarely said anything good about Memphis. On April 3, 1968, the SCLC lawyers appeared in federal court in Memphis in the same building where Jamie worked. His IRS office was on the first floor and the federal court was on the 11th floor. Jamie rode up in the elevator with Dr. King and the SCLC lawyers that morning. The federal court issued an injunction which prohibited the City of Memphis from blocking the March. It was a victory for the SCLC and a defeat for the City of Memphis. That night Dr. King appeared in the large auditorium of the Masonic Temple before an enthusiastic audience, which included Jamie, to speak about the struggle. Dr. King was a great speaker and Jamie had brought Donna and the kids to hear the speech. Dr. King told the crowd in a passionate voice " I have been to the Mountaintop and I am not afraid to die" "I'm not fearing any man" The crowd rocked the Church with cheers.

April 4th, 1968 was a cool clear day in Memphis. Dr. King and other leaders of the SCLC were staying at a black owned motel, the Lorraine Motel. During previous visits Dr. King and the SCLC had been guests at the much nicer Holiday Inn Rivermont. The Holiday Inn Rivermont sat on a river bluff overlooking the Mississippi with no other buildings near it. The Lorraine Motel sat in a cluttered neighborhood in South Memphis not far from Beale Street. It was not nearly as nice as the Rivermont. Dr. King and the SCLC would have preferred to have been staying at the Rivermont but some people had been critical of the group for staying at a white owned Hotel when they could have stayed in the black community in a black owned motel. Just west of the Lorraine Motel sat a cheap, brick rooming house which offered cheap rooms to white transients. The Lorraine is a two story building with an open outside walkway connecting the rooms. On that April 4th day Dr. King was relaxing as he prepared for a speech he was planning to give that night. He was tired and melancholy. Sometimes the stress got to him. The constant threats of death. The constant travel and the many speeches and meetings he attended sometimes left him exhausted. Where ever he went people wanted to hear him talk, or they wanted to touch him. Shake his hand. In his speech the night before he had said that they, his people, would someday make it to the mountaintop to the promised land of equality and opportunity but that he might not make it with them. He knew that he was under constant, twenty four hour surveillance by the FBI. He knew that the FBI bugged his phone, his car, his room. What he didn't know is that on this particular day the Director of the FBI, J Edgar Hoover, who despised him, had ordered that this surveillance cease for a few hours. Across from the Lorraine Motel, in a shabby dirty room a man stood on a bathtub with a rifle aimed across to the Lorraine. When the man saw Dr. King walking along the corridor he aimed his rifle at Dr. King's head. He aimed his rifle at a man who had won the Nobel Peace Prize, the foremost advocate of non violence in the United States, the idol of millions of people, the unchallenged leader of the American Civil Rights movement and one of the most charismatic speakers in the world. The man who J. Edgar Hoover hated and wanted dead. The man pulled the trigger and the bullet killed the dreamer. It killed the man of peace. As he died his voice was stilled and he passed into history. He became a martyr for the cause of civil rights. He became a martyr for the garbage men of Memphis. The FBI operative who had murdered Dr. King was never found. J. Edgar Hoover had hired the assassin and had agreed to pay him $30,000. The man was told to meet Hoover at a farmhouse near Washington, D.C. which was Hoover's weekend retreat. Two days after the assassination the man met Hoover and Hoover's lover Clyde Tolan. Hoover congratulated the man and while the man was accepting the congratulations Hoover produced a 38 pistol from his pocket and shot the man in the middle of his forehead. The body was placed in a furnace stocked with dry wood, pulp paper and coal and the paper was lit with a match. In a short time the man's body was nothing but ashes. Afterwards Hoover returned to Washington, D.C. to "direct" the search for the assassin of Dr. King.

The death of Dr. King, while it delighted J.Edgar Hoover, stunned and saddened the world. Some were stunned by the loss of someone who preached non violence. Others were stunned by the loss of a pivotal figure in American life; an eloquent speaker; a man of influence, a man who could inspire. Many others simply felt that they had lost a friend. Still others were just plain angry. They showed that anger in the streets and alleys of cities all across the U.S. by rioting and burning. Many people died and many more were arrested. In Memphis, ironically, the Invaders who disliked Dr. King and the non violence he preached, sparked the first riots. They began sniping at police cars with rifles. Near a black housing project a young black man was shot to death by police.

In Memphis, Mayor Loeb's main regret was not that Dr. King had been killed but that he had been killed in Memphis. Gloom and fear settled over the country. Many predicted wide spread and continued strife. The body of Dr. King was returned to Atlanta and he was buried. His funeral service was held in the Church from which he had preached for freedom, equality and non violence. One of the more memorable eulogies was presented by Robert F. Kennedy. Two weeks after his death, a March in his honor was held in Memphis. It was more of a memorial than anything else. It was attended by more than

50000 people and it was peaceful.

The City of Memphis was tainted for ever. Even Mayor Loeb and those whites who had supported now wanted to settle the strike immediately. The strike was settled.

Jamie's support of the strike had further angered many powerful people. The powerful congressman who represented Memphis was after his job and people were circulating petitions to have him fired. The IRS in fact fired him for a short time but were forced to re-instate him when 3000 IRS Revenue Officers in 20 states called in sick after he was fired. He was immediately re-instated. However, Dr. King's death had a deep impression on Jamie. He no longer wanted to live in Memphis. The memories were too painful and he feared for the safety of his family. He continued to receive threats. An FBI agent who Jamie often talked with at lunch in the federal building had come to Jamie and slipped him a cassette tape. The tape was a recording of a bugging devise which the FBI had planted in Jamie's house. Jamie listened to the tape and among other things heard a conversation he and Donna had one night, while laying in their bed, about how the kids were doing in school. It was time for Jamie to leave Memphis. Out of the blue he received a telephone call from someone with whom he had worked when he was working at the Pentagon. He now worked for IBM and wanted to know if Jamie would be willing to come to work for IBM at a research facility in New York City.

Chapter 13-Osama bin Laden

The bin Ladens had served the House of Saud since its modern day founder, Muhammad bin Oud bin Laden had earned the gratitude of King Ibn Saud by building a road which made it easier for the old King to reach the second floor of his vast palace. In 1964, upon the death of King ibn Saud, the new King, Faysal, rewarded the bin Ladens by giving them a contract to build a network of roads in the Kingdom. In 1973 the bin

Laden family was given a massive contract to rebuild the holy sites at Mecca and Medina. It was said that Muhammad bin Laden used the wealth and power which came his way to marry eleven wives during his lifetime. Osama's mother was a Syrian while most of the other wives were Saudi or Yemeni. Over the years the bin Ladens continued to work for the House of Saud and they owed the vast wealth they accumulated to the House of Saud. The bin Ladens also worked with several U.S. governments and it was rumored that one of Osama's half brothers, Salem bin Laden had served the Reagan administration by secretly arranging for 34 million dollars to be funneled through Saudi Arabia to the Nicaraguan Contras.

Salem bin Laden was one of the closest friends of the Saudi King and had close friendships with many American diplomats and businessmen.

By 2001 the House of Saud, and the rest of the Saudi establishment had created the fiction that Osama was an outcast and that he was an enemy of the House of Saud. This fiction was made transparent by the continued patronage of the bin Laden family by the House of Saud. In 2001, In Saudi Arabia, where public opinion is influenced and tightly controlled by the House of Saud, Osama bin Laden was a hero. He continued to receive millions of dollars from the House of Saud and the bin Ladens continued to enjoy the favor and money of the House of Saud.

Osama bin Laden espoused the same Islamic beliefs of the House of Saud, Wahhabism.

In 1998, Osama bin Laden, who had received both money and military support from the U.S. in the fight to run the Soviets out of Afghanistan, declared a *jihad* against the United States. In his call for *Jihad* Osama called for holy war against the United States. This holy war sanctioned attacks on Americans wherever they were.

Osama, on behalf of the House of Saud, became public enemy number one for the United States. However, in Saudi Arabia, most surveys of the Saudi people indicated that Osama bin Laden had the support and admiration of 90% of the people. Posters with his picture appeared in every Saudi school and in the homes of most Saudi citizens. In public, members of the House of Saud continued to insist that the attacks of 9/ 11 were the work of Zionists. After 9/11 the US. Launched an intensive search for Osama bin Laden. At first the search focused on the mountains of Afghanistan but bin Laden could not be found. Eventually the US teacked him to a town in Pakistan where he was being hidden by the Pakistani. A group of U.S. Navy Seals killed him and dropped his corpse into the Ocean.

Chapter 14- New York City and modeling for Macys

IBM was doing research on how to use the huge computers which were being used to accumulate, categorize and dispense information. Jamie found a nice house in Brooklyn which was a short distance from a subway station which Jamie could use to go back and forth to work. Donna liked the house very much and immediately proceeded to make it a good home for Jamie, Cindy and the new baby. His job at IBM was exciting. IBM had developed a think tank to look at computers and how they could be used in a business environment. The office from which Jamie worked was in mid- Manhattan in the garment district and Jamie liked the hustle and bustle. Once a week Donna would leave the children with an Italian woman who lived next door to them and come to Manhattan to have lunch. On about her second visit to Manhattan she was waiting for Jamie at a small corner coffee shop with a stand up lunch counter. As she stood at the counter having a glass of iced tea a well dressed man who looked to be about 50 came up to Donna and asked her if she had ever done any modeling. Donna gave her usual response that she was married and a stay at home mother to two children. The man said he worked for Macy's, which was two blocks away and he suggested to Donna that she come by and see him at the store. Donna was often approached by men and like most Southern women she could handle such approaches with a friendly but firm rejection. When Jamie arrived she showed him the man's card and he immediately suggested they walk over to Macy's and see what it was all about. When they reached the man's office at Macys the man came out and invited them into his office. He immediately offered Donna a job as a print media model, modeling bras, panties and negligees. In the ads which would be used in newspapers and magazines Donna's face would not be shown. When the man told them how much the modeling assignments would pay they were both flabbergasted. Jamie immediately recommended to Donna that she accept the job. The Italian woman who lived next to them, who adored Cindy and the baby, would be glad to baby sit when Donna was on modeling assignments. Shortly thereafter Donna became a

model and Jamie began seeing a familiar shape as he read the

newspaper on the way into work. The photographers loved

having Donna as a model. She looked good from any angle

and had the sort of shape that made any bra, panty or

negligee look good. A few weeks after she began her

modeling career Macys asked if she would consider

becoming a runway model modeling bras, panties and

negligees for wholesale buyers. The thought of appearing on

a runway dressed in a bra and panty or in a negligee made

Donna nervous. However, Jamie pointed out that she

wouldn't be showing any more skin than in a bathing suit at

the beach. Donna quickly became one of the more sought

after runway models for Macys. When she was scheduled to

model the number of buyers attending always was more than

double the usual number. The exposure she received created

even more interest. She was asked to pose in a Playboy

Magazine spread as part of

an article about runway models. However, Playboy wanted her to pose nude. This was too much for Donna and she refused. She was also receiving offers from other modeling agencies to appear as a model for print and TV ads. After six months in New York City Donna was the toast of the town. Jamie enjoyed his work with IBM and he enjoyed the attention Donna was receiving. He had always told her she was beautiful and all the attention Donna was receiving proved that he wasn't the only one who thought so.

IBM was really impressed by Jamie's ability to quickly analyze projects. They asked Jamie if he would be willing to go to work for them in a huge research facility they had in Southern England. Before agreeing to do so Jamie went home to discuss the move with Donna. He knew she was enjoying life in New York City. To his surprise Donna did not hesitate and quickly agreed to move to England.

Chapter 15-*Passing the Deadly Plans*

Shortly after the New Year, the Lord traveled to the United States as he often did. He visited several cities on the East Coast including Boston, New York City and Washington, D.C. He was doing the footwork for his plan to attack the United States. During his visit the Lord had lunch at the famed World Trade Center restaurant- Windows on the World, from which he could see many miles over the area. He knew that the World Trade Center played an important part in the commercial life of the United States and that it was a symbol of American wealth. The Lord also visited Washington, D.C. where he was a guest of the Secretary of the Treasury at a formal lunch at the Treasury Department near the White House. The Lord had previously been a guest at the White House during several prior visits.

When the Lord returned to London he prepared a simple plan to begin the secret war against the United States.

The plan would involve the closely coordinated hijacking of ten commercial airliners from the airports of Boston, Washington, D.C., Newark, Philadelphia and Cleveland with full loads of passengers and full loads of jet fuel. None of the hijackings would begin until time enough had passed for all ten airliners to be in the air. Each group of hijackers would include two trained pilots and four musclemen to take and hold control of the airliners. Two of the airliners would proceed to strike the upper floors of the world trade center. One would hit Rockefeller Center, One would strike the Empire State Building, One would strike the Pentagon, One would strike the White House, Two would strike the U.S. Capitol, One would strike the US State Department and one would strike the headquarters of the CIA. The plan was very specific in terms of the number of people required and the amount of money needed to complete the project. The Lord prepared the plan, in Arabic, using a Power Point presentation on his computer. Once the plan was complete it was given to one of the many bin Laden family members who was going to school in London. She took the plan to a cousin in Yemen who gave it to another cousin who took it to Osama bin Laden. The Lord provided the plan and Osama provided the people. The House of Saud, through the House of bin Laden, provided the money. Wahhabism provided the fanaticism. By the time the plan got to bin Laden the purpose of the attack was to advance the *Jihad* previously declared by Osama. A very sophisticated suicide attack . No one in the House of Saud or the House of bin Laden knew the real reason why the attacks were to be made. If there was to be a world government they wanted it to be one ruled by the Wahhabist. They thought the attacks had to do with the advance of Islam, the advance of Wahhabism.

Say what you may about the organization of Osama bin Laden. It was secure. No leaks. Osama and his followers had gone to great lengths to check the loyalties of all those involved in planning the 9/11 attacks on the U.S. Not a single key member of the group training to carry out the attacks was an agent for any intelligence agency. The key members of the sub groups created to carry out the tasks were those who would serve as pilots. Most members of the ten teams were Saudis or Yemenis and could expect to have easy access to the U.S. It would not be necessary for any of them to sneak into the U.S. They did not need to look for a side door to enter the U.S. As Saudis they could come right in the front door. It was not unusual for Saudis to come to the U.S. for pilot training. In fact thousands of Saudis had been trained as pilots in the U.S. with many of them trained by the U.S. Air Force. Flight schools liked to train the Saudis. Always plenty of money and always easy to train. The members of the ten groups didn't need to spend time making or finding explosives. The jet fuel on the planes would be all they needed. They didn't need to worry about smuggling guns onto the plane. All they needed was surprise, teamwork, muscle, a few knives and a few sharp instruments. It was a simple plan. Much less complicated than the Japanese plans for Pearl Harbor.

During the training Osama built a facility which contained a detailed replica of a commercial jet liners interior complete with seats, a cockpit, overhead bins, etc. and all of the team members were frequent fliers.

By September 11, 2001 the teams were ready. As the day approached Osama cancelled three of the teams. Some members of these two teams seemed a bit nervous about dying and weren't reassured that they would become instant martyrs and go directly to heaven. Two other teams had suffered training accidents and were not able to make the trip to the U.S.

On the morning of September 11th another one of the teams lost their nerve at the last moment and didn't make their scheduled flights. However, on the morning of September 11th four of Osama's teams made their flights. Three of the flights hit their targets.

236

Chapter 16-England and IBM

Jamie and his family settled in Southern England in the city of Southampton not far from IBM's research facility and Jamie continued to do research for IBM. Donna began taking modeling assignments in London but would only accept assignments which would allow her to go back to Southampton for the night.

Jamie's work at the IBM research facility totally absorbed his life but he still found time to spend evenings and weekends with Donna and their two children. By now Cindy had become a beautiful blue eyed blond whose good looks supplemented that of Donna when the family was out in public. Cindy was attending school in Southampton where she was very popular with her teachers and classmates. On weekends the family would travel throughout the Island. To Winchester to tour the town and it's cathedral. To Salisbury Plain to see Stonehenge. To Bath to see the ruins of the wall built by the Romans. To

Glasgow, Edinburgh and the highlands to see Scotland. To the hills and mountains of Wales. To Liverpool to see the industrial North. To London to see all the sights of the many boroughs which make up Metro London. Once they had seen the Island they ventured further a field to see France, Belgium, the Netherlands, Sweden, Norway, Switzerland, Germany, Denmark, Spain, Portugal, Turkey, Greece. Every weekend the family went somewhere to see more of the world.

These were exciting times for Jamie and for IBM. Jamie had always admitted IBM. " Big Blue" had developed a computer language, Fortran, based on Algebra, grammar and syntax which Jamie had learned as a young man. At the time Fortran was the language used to program computers. IBM had just developed the floppy disk which opened many doors for those, like Jamie, who were working to develop computers. Jamie's research team was working to develop a smaller computer to replace the behemoths which were so large that they could fill a large warehouse. The goal was to develop computer storage capability which would fit in a computer small enough to be carried by a single person. The research team was finishing the testing of the IBM 5100 computer. At nearly 50 pounds the IBM 5100 was the forerunner of the Personal Computer. Computer also need to have codes to run them and Jamie spent much of his time developing codes and operating procedures.

Donna's modeling career permitted she and Jamie to take many trips throughout Europe which were paid by the modeling agencies who wanted to photograph Donna's beauty. She would only take weekend assignments and would only come to a photo session if she could bring Jamie and the kids. The Italians and French clamored for Donna to be photographed for fashion layouts in Rome or Paris. She appeared in billboards all over England and Europe, She was finicky about what she would agree to be photographed with. She wouldn't appear in cigarette ads and she wouldn't appear for products that she didn't really use. Because of her modeling career and the notoriety she attracted she and Jamie attending many fashionable events. Jamie was always amused to see the way photographers fawned over Donna. He knew she was beautiful and he was always glad for her beauty to be recognized.

After almost three years in England Jamie and Donna were homesick to return to the United States. They thought about returning to New York or Memphis but instead they decided to return to Jamie's original hometown, Urbana.

Chapter 17 The new Caliphate

After the 911 attack the U.S. invaded Afghanistan whose rulers followed the same version of Islam as did Saudi Arabia. In addition based on faulty intelligence the U.S. invaded Iraq to remove Sadaam

Hussein. His army was quickly routed and replaced by a

Shite government favored by the U.S. After the defeat of the

Iraqi Army the U.S. allowed the new government in Baghdad

to purge the Iraqi army of Sunni who constituted most of the

officer corp of the army. The new Shite government of Iraq

forced the U.S. military to withdraw from Iraq. After the

withdrawal of the U.S. military the Shite government of Iraq

began a savage campaign to remove Sunni from all positions

of power. During this same period Syrian rebels continued to

try to overthrow the Syrian government of Bashar Al Assad.

They were supported by the U.S. They managed to seize a

portion of Syria, In the meantime a power vacuum occurred

in a large portion of Iraq where many Sunni tribes lived.

These tribes had been badly mistreated by the Shite

government of Baghdad. They combined with the Syrian

rebels and seized a portion of Syria and Iraq and formed what

they called a Caliphate. The

new "Caliphate" was based upon the same 13th Century version of Islam which the rulers of Saudi Arabia followed. The Iraqi based in Baghdad ceded much of the Sunni area they controlled. Instead of fighting the new Caliphate which the West began calling the "Islamic State of Iraq and the Levant or ISIL," the Iraqi abandoned the weapons they had been provided by the US and fled back to Baghdad. ISIL received millions of dollars and thousands of men from Saudi Arabia. The new Caliphate decided to use a campaign of terror to subdue those who lived in the Caliphate. They murdered thousands of people and in a short time they earned the opposition of almost every country in the world. They were able to begin pumping oil from the area they controlled which they sold in the international market through Saudi Arabia. After the formation of their Caliphate, ISIL continued to receive weapons and supplies through support from Saudi Arabia and Turkey. They also began receiving recruits from all over the world attracted by their extreme version of Islam. In the meantime Saudi Arabia made a decision to annex the territory controlled by the new Caliphate and return Saudi Arabia to control of radical Islam. Although much of the world had opposed ISIL the world accepted the new and larger Saudi Arabia and its Islamic extremism.

Chapter 18- Jamie's Revenge

The years of work Jamie had completed left him with a long list of those he was going to punish. He had gotten to know many of the members of the House of Saud. He disliked many of them but he also liked a few of them. He had completed many months of research to try to identify those who had participated in any way in the planning or financing of the attacks on the U.S. or who supported the radical Islam of the newly enlarged Saudi Arabia. He did not plan to kill Saudis merely because they cheered the attacks on the U.S. but he did plan to rob the Saudis of the wealth which formed the basis for their indolent life styles. The list of Saudis that he planned to kill was a fairly short list. It included some members of the House of Saud and some members of the House of bin Laden. He did not need to include bin Laden on his list. The U.S. military had managed to kill bin Laden and his leadership core through drone strikes and an attack on bin Laden where he was hiding in Pakistan.. He also included on his list a group of clerics who were preaching and teaching the particularly virulent brew of Wahhabism. These clerics were instrumental in fostering the climate of hatred which had produced men like the Saudis who had hijacked the planes carrying innocent people on 9/11. They were also the basis for the Caliphate formed by ISIL.

What did Jamie plan to do to get his revenge? He planned to kill almost 300 Saudis. He planned to sabotage the Saudi capacity to produce oil He planned to wipe out all of the wealth of the House of Saud and the House of bin Laden's.

He planned to personally kill the Lord. He planned to satisfy the feelings of Rage which motivated him every day.

Chapter 19 –The Invisible Rich Man

After Jamie moved his family back to Urbana, Illinois he entered the University of Illinois where he studied computer science. These were exciting times for computer nerds. The personal computer was revolutionizing how data was accumulated and how it was stored. The computer was not just a machine used to make calculations. It was not just a machine which would permit more rapid ways of dealing with numbers. It was a device which permitted the storage and rapid access of knowledge.

When he was ready Jamie founded his own company to develop software programs for use by large companies and governments. After developing and patenting a number of trail blazing procedures Jamie sold his company for six billion dollars. He gave half of this to the employees who had helped him build his company. He immediately started another company to develop information technology software and middleware programs. He also invested in a number of companies including a new company known as Microsoft and in the retail company Wal-Mart. He had met Sam Walton, the founder of Wal-Mart, at a computer show where Walton was trying to find a better way of tracking inventory. Walton was just eccentric enough to attract the admiration of Jamie.

By 1980 Jamie was a very rich man but he didn't live like a rich man. He lived in a modest home in a small farming community in Central Illinois from which he managed his vast wealth. Jamie didn't have the life style of a rich man. His home was comfortable but no one in his hometown suspected that Jamie was a very rich man. He attracted very little attention in the area. Both of his grandfathers had farmed in the same area for many years and Jamie knew most of the families in the area. The two story house was more than 80 years old and had been built during a time when families were large. It had once been the home of a farmer with a big family and was on a 640 acre tract of farmland which still produced corn and soybeans. After Jamie bought the house he leased the farmland out to one of his cousins. Not even his cousin had any idea how rich Jamie really was. Jamie didn't flaunt his wealth and never had more than a few thousand dollars in the local bank. Jamie remodeled the house. He did most of the work himself with the help of his two children and his cousin. He expanded the basement and raised the foundation of the house just a bit to make it possible to add a small indoor swimming pool in the basement. On the first floor Jamie built a large office for himself with a large bay window with two way glass looking out over the fields which surrounded the house. He also installed a beautiful modern kitchen, a den and family room with a large fireplace and study rooms for his son and daughter. The second floor contained bedrooms for he, Donna and the two children and four extra bedrooms for guests. Around the outside of the second floor was a porch which went all around the house. The porch contained swinging benches on which the family could sit and watch television when the weather was nice. Or, if they so chose, they could sit and swing in the swings and watch the corn grow. Outside of the house were a couple of outbuildings one of which contained Jamie's workshop where he liked to build or take apart computers and other electronic devices. The property also contained two large windmills which generated electricity. Jamie had installed solar collectors and with these and the windmills his house generated all of its' own electricity. In addition the property included an old well house and the well provided all the water the family could use. He had converted an old barn into an indoor basketball / tennis court. He and his wife, Donna, didn't have servants and their two children, Cindy, born in 1963 and Jimmy, born in

1966, went to the public school system. As he had gained wealth Jamie went to great lengths to hide it. He never owned more than three cars, an Olds 98 which he drove, an Olds Cutlass which Donna drove and a Chevrolet Camaro which he had bought for his daughter when she reached her 16th birthday. He traded cars every two years. He also had an old pickup truck that he used to haul things around and a tractor to help tend the half acre garden the family maintained. The family also had a small orchard with apple and cherry trees. In addition they had a large, climate controlled greenhouse in which Jamie grew oranges, lemons, bananas and other hot weather plants. He paid his cousin's children to help him maintain the plants and trees in the greenhouse. Like the rest of the complex the electricity for the greenhouse came from solar collectors and windmills. He and Donna had furnished their house by attending estate auctions throughout Central Illinois. Jamie didn't have any of the habits of a rich man. Their were many homes in the area at least as nice, from the outside, as Jamies, but none of them had the sort of sophisticated computer and communications systems found in Jamies house. He didn't gamble and like his father before him he was a lifelong teetotaler. He didn't own a Rolex watch. His Casio cost $20.00 and kept excellent time. He didn't have a private jet but he did own a small Piper Cub which he liked to fly on weekends throughout the area. He kept it housed at a small local airport.

He had formed many off shore companies through which he managed his wealth and he maintained contact with those who worked for him through the office in his home. The office in his home was off limits to outsiders. It had windows through which Jamie could see out but through which no one could see in. The perimeter of the house had an elaborate security system which included a twelve foot high cyclone fence around the outside perimeter and an eight foot brick wall around the house and yard. Between the outside fence and the brick wall, both of which were covered by vines, Jamie had three large dogs. The dogs, two yellow labs and a collie, were friendly but barked anytime a stranger came on the property. Just outside the cyclone fence which enclosed the five acres of Jamie's house and out buildings was a farmhouse in which his cousin, a farmer, his wife and three children lived. His cousin farmed Jamie's farm. The farmhouse also had a beautiful swimming pool covered by a Plexiglas cover so that it was possible for the two families to swim regardless of the weather. The farmhouse and its' out buildings was enclosed by a second 12 foot high cyclone fence also covered by vines. His cousin also had a couple of large dogs which roamed his area.

To get to the two houses and their outbuildings it was necessary to come up a quarter of a mile driveway from the county road that came by the property. A gate at the front of the driveway blocked entry to the driveway. Entry could be made through an intercom system which connected the gate with the two main houses. A hidden camera was trained on the entrance gate through which those in either of the houses could see any one seeking entry. Access to Jamie's house didn't require that he drive through the portion of the complex containing his cousin's house.

Over the years Jamie had established a number of bank accounts in Switzerland and in banks in other countries with bank account secrecy protection. He also had regular bank accounts in the U.S. but used these like petty cash accounts to pay living expenses. He never kept much money in the local bank but he had other accounts in Chicago with larger sums of money. He also had many bank accounts in foreign countries including each of the eleven countries where he owned companies. In the basement of Jamie's house was a safe in which he kept a small fortune in gold, silver and diamonds. Jamie was one of the richest men in the U.S. but his name didn't appear on any lists of wealthy men. He paid his taxes but most of his net worth was held in the many companies that he owned. Most of his wealth remained in his companies and wasn't distributed to Jamie. The companies paid corporate taxes and rarely distributed dividends to Jamie. This permitted him to accumulate wealth without having it in his own name. Jamie had established an elaborate maze of companies so that even the best researcher couldn't track his wealth. He had nearly two billion dollars which he held in various locations in gold, silver or platinum. He maintained a hundred million dollars in his many bank accounts so that he had adequate liquidity if he wanted to buy or start a new company based on his personal research.

In 1985 Jamie began buying residences in a number of countries which helped him satisfy his gypsy instincts. By 1986 he and Donna were living parts of the year in other countries. They lived

January and February in a modest apartment in Hong Kong. March and April were spent in a modest home in North London. In May and June they lived in a modest home in a small town in the Black Forest area of Germany. In July and August they lived in a modest home near Helsinki, Finland. In September and October they lived in a modest home in Nova Scotia. In November and December they were always in their home in Central Illinois. During their times away from Central Illinois their home was locked and watched over by Jamie's cousin and his family. The cousin would take care of Jamie's pets which, in addition to dogs included several families of cats, a couple of goats and a couple of horses. By now both of Jamie's children had left home to attend college.

Over the years Jamie had accumulated many cadres of employees to help him manage his many businesses. Each of these cadres was independent of the other. Jamie paid his employees well and he demanded that they respect his privacy. Jamie had developed very tight controls over his companies so he could always know what was going on in each of them. He required daily progress reports and monthly financial reports. He had developed a sophisticated reporting system which allowed him to access the financial data bases of each of his companies anytime he wanted to do so. He also kept track of all of the employees of his companies although they numbered more than 20,000 people in 11 countries. He required that all of his companies maintain a detailed profile on each of his employees which included things like birthplaces, cultural background, languages spoken, education, family information, and hobbies. He personally reviewed the profiles of every employee hired and he took pride in the fact that his employees were the best available. He paid his employees very well and provided benefits far exceeding that of other employers. He reimbursed his employees for continuing

255

education, provided scholarships for their children, provided medical and dental care of the best quality. He also allowed his employees to take part in profit sharing plans and rewarded employees who developed new ideas, helped improve company products or developed new products. Many of his employees were scientists and leaders in their particular areas of expertise.. Jamie was an extremely paternalistic employer.

Some of his companies would make a steady profit without much growth. Others would lose money as they developed products or technology. Some of his most valuable companies never made profits but accumulated products, technologies or patents of great value. Once a company reached a certain size Jamie would sell it and invest the proceeds in new companies. Because Jamie was a risk taker some of the companies he started failed but most were profitable and very successful. All of his companies were tied in some way to high technology, (computer and information technology, the world wide web and related industries.) Jamie had started companies all over the world but he was partial to several companies, despite high taxes, he had started in Canada and in Finland.

Jamie had five employees who he had met and worked with over the years who were men he trusted completely and who helped him manage what eventually became his worldwide business empire. They were his most trusted friends and he had made each one of them very rich.

Jamie had met John Devore in High School where they played on the high school football team. John had gone on after high school to attend the Naval Academy in Annapolis, MD and had risen to the rank of Captain during his Naval career. Like Jamie he had married his high school sweetheart and over the years Jamie and John had remained close friends. In 1985 Jamie hired John to help him run a small company in Wisconsin to develop and sell robotic devices. The company developed and manufactured robotic devices some of which were used in various manufacturing processes and some of which had military applications. This included the manufacture of drones which operated much like model airplanes but which had capabilities far beyond a typical model airplane.

Jamie had met Dave Mandrell during his college days. Dave had gone on to get a degree in electrical engineering with an emphasis upon radio technology. Jamie had purchased a small company based in Finland which was developing satellites for use in radio communications and ran a satellite radio company. The company had paid eighty million dollars in 1993 to put a satellite into space and was a leader in satellite communications. Dave seemed like a natural choice to run this company for Jamie and after re-locating to Finland he quickly learned to speak Finnish.

Jamie had met George Thornton during the time he had lived and worked in

England. At that time George worked for IBM at a large research facility in Southern England. He and Jamie played on the same amateur basketball team in Southampton. At 6-4 George might have been a good basketball player except for the fact that he was flat footed and couldn't jump more than a few inches. However, George, like Jamie, was a fierce competitor. After Jamie had purchased a British software/middleware company he hired George to help him run it and in a few years the company was a leading provider of computer applications used in information technology.

Jamie had met Bill Morgan during his time in Vietnam. Bill was a Chief Warrant Office who had been working as a Crane Operator in a giant lift helicopter(the CH-54 Flying Crane) Jamie had once saved Bill Morgan's life and Bill was extremely grateful. In 1989 Jamie had purchased a German aeronautical engineering company and Bill Morgan was the Manager of this company for Jamie. Bill re-located to Germany and   learned to speak German.

Jamie had met Weldon Roberts in Nova Scotia in 1990. Weldon was a large man, 6-6, who had developed an advanced interest in Nano Technology and in 1992 he had persuaded Jamie to buy a Canadian company which was a pioneer in Nano Technology. All of Jamie's companies spent much of their time to develop or enhance what could be called cutting edge technology.

By September 11, 2001, Jamie was one of the richest men in the world but he continued to live a modest life style. When he flew from place to place he always flew coach class on the same airline. He owned a majority share in this airline but none of the airline employees knew that this coach passenger owned most of the airline. Because he was a frequent flier he always managed to get a seat in coach in front of the bulkhead where he could stretch his legs. If the flight wasn't full he usually was seated in an empty row. He knew enough about the computer seat assignment system to manipulate it a bit. When he got wherever he was going Jamie rented a car and if he was flying to some place with which he was not familiar he usually hired a driver to drive him. He often would rent a small plane to go sightseeing when he was in a new area and had the time. When he traveled he almost always took Donna with him. Wherever he went he carried his laptop and other communications aids. He always had the latest technology.

After September 11, 2001 it quickly became clear that the best place to look for those who had planned and financed the attack of that date was Saudi Arabia. One of the companies that Jamie owned provided sophisticated computer services to the House of Saud. Accordingly, Jamie got him self hired as a research technician for that company and he moved to Saudi Arabia.

After the attack in Chicago Jamie had returned to his home in Southern Illinois. He had buried caskets for each of his murdered family members in a small cemetery in Central Illinois. There were no bodies to put in each of the caskets and so he had placed in them photos and personal items of each of his loved ones. In his wife's' casket he had placed photos of her when she was a girl of eight, photos of he and she at her Senior Prom, a copy of their wedding license, her Senior High School yearbook; a photo of she and Jamie with Elvis Presley standing in front of Graceland's front door; photos of Donna's parents and of their two children. He had also placed in the casket letters he had sent to Donna when he had been in Vietnam and other letters he had written her over the years. He also included a book of Donna's favorite poems and the wedding dress she had worn the day they were married. He had also arranged for a local florist to place a dozen roses on her grave every Monday morning. It hurt him very much and renewed his rage that there was nothing left of Donna anywhere in the world except for his memories of her

In the days and weeks after the attacks of 2007 Jamie spent most of his time sitting in front of his computer accessing the world's largest library(the Internet). Through one of his companies he had access to top secret reports from the CIA, the NSA and the FBI regarding their investigations into the attacks. Within a week after the massacre it was apparent to Jamie that the answers concerning who had planned, financed and carried out the attacks would be found in Saudi Arabia.

Chapter 20- Trump and the State of the Union

As time had passed a different type of President was elected. He had built a fortune in real estate and by licensing his name for many things. He had developed a popular reality TV program whose punch line was "Your Fired". He had been elected by winning a majority of the Electoral College even while losing the popular vote. He was a large man with a high profile fashion model as his wife. He was crude and lewd which seemed to endear him to his base of support. He managed to offend large numbers of people. Most of the media searched for bad things to say about him. He was accused of links with Russia and it was said that the Russians had helped elect him. He had visited Saudi Arabia to great fanfare and had been presented with a large gold necklace by King Salman.. .

It had all begun with an attack during the Presidents' annual State of the Union speech. As the President began his speech a deadly, colorless, odorless poison gas flowed into the chamber through the heating vents and everyone in the great hall was dead in less than two minutes. TV images of the scene were beamed around the world from cameras manned by dead camera crews. The new President of the United States, who had succeeded to office as provided by the U.S. constitution upon the assassinations of the President and Vice President, declared martial law. She had been purposely required not to attend the State of the Union speech since it was felt that someone in the line of succession should be kept out of possible harm's way. Without that foresight the United States would have been left without a President. After the massacre at the State of the Union gathering, the new President had taken over. She had been taken to a secure facility in West Virginia where she sought to govern a country experiencing a power vacuum like none other in history. She had no Congress to assist her or impede the directives she issued. At this point in U.S. history the portion of the U.S. constitution which spoke of separation of powers meant nothing. All nine members of the Supreme Court had died in the attack and only three members of Congress had survived.

Shortly after the State of the Union attack the United States suffered hundreds of coordinated attacks on its' oil and gas pipelines and the destruction of much of its electrical grid system. State governments and the federal government were largely unprepared for the loss of fuel and electricity. Of course, few Americans were prepared for the loss of fuel and electricity. The primary problem concerned food production and food distribution.

Americans were accustomed to having things like orange juice and lemonade but with no fuel and no electricity to harvest, process and distribute food the country was thrown into a desperate struggle to feed people. Trucks, trains and planes could not move food. Cities, in particular, were descending into chaos. Businesses were unable to operate. Factories closed since workers couldn't get to work and factories didn't have the fuel or electricity needed to stay open. Aid poured into the United States from all over the world but piled up in ports on the East Coast and West Coast. The federal government's strategic fuel reserves lasted only a week and it was not used by the government in an efficient matter. Within a day of the loss of electricity in most cities supermarket shelves were bare. China sent the US 500,000 bicycles. The Canadian and Mexican government set up refugee centers into which came hundreds of thousands of Americans. Within a day of the national power outages riots broke out in every major

U.S. city. Looters controlled cities and law enforcement was non existence. It took government almost three weeks to establish food and water distribution points. Canada and Mexico shipped in fifty million bottles of bottled water but getting it distributed was difficult. Hospitals couldn't operate and medical care for those with serious injuries or illnesses ceased to exist. The newly installed President directed that all available fuel go to military reserve and national guard units. Fortunately some vehicles could operate on battery power for short distances. The first priority was to regain control of the cities and to feed those unfortunate enough to live in an American city. In many rural areas people were able to get by because they were close to where food was grown.

Thousands of people in rural areas helped harvest food and get it to cities by bicycle or with horse drawn farm wagons. But for every thousand people in the country there were a 100,000 in the cities who didn't grow any sort of food. City people had depended upon fuel and power to get to work, access their money, buy food and get water. Water purification and distribution systems in the cities depended upon fuel and electricity. It took the government almost 2 months before it was able to begin restoring electricity to most cities. Some smaller towns had never lost their electricity because they were independent of the massive power grids but every area, small town and rural areas, were devastated by the loss of fuel. Farmers couldn't run their tractors. Food canners couldn't operate their canneries. Food was pouring into the U.S. from all over the world but getting it distributed was a major problem. Bicycles became one of the major means of transportation. Jamie had been in constant touch with his cousin through a satellite feed. His cousin and his family were safe on the farm. They still had electricity and the years supply of bio fuel they had on the property allowed them to operate their farm machinery and, with the coming of Spring, plant corn and soybeans on their 640 acres. Jamie had more than a years worth of food stored on the farm and it fed his family and many of his neighbors as they fought to survive the winter.

With Spring most families planted much larger gardens than usual.

Chapter 21- **The Biggest Heist in History**

It was time for Jamie to take his revenge. He had drawn up a plan under which he would do the following:

(1) Use his computer skills and the knowledge he had accumulated during the last four years to redistribute all of the wealth the House of bin Laden and House of Saud had accumulated over the years. Much of the wealth of the bin Ladens and the Saudi was in stocks, bonds, and certificates of deposits scattered all over the world. Jamie had used his computer skills to identify where and how securities and c.d's were held. Banks and brokerage firms rely on a complex system of

authorizations based upon documentations. Stocks,

bonds and certificates of deposits and other funds in

other types of accounts can be transferred with the

proper authorizations. Quite often ownership

transfers could be done by computer. Ownership of

stocks, bonds, certificates of deposits and bank

accounts could readily be moved from one owner to

another. If Jamie had sold these stocks and bonds or

withdrawn the huge sums of cash from c.d.'s or other

bank accounts, companies would fail, banks would

fail and in some cases, governments would fall.

However, Jamie had developed a computer program

which would allow him to irreversibly change

ownership of the fortunes accumulated by the Houses

of bin Laden and Saud. He also knew through his

complete access to the thousands of financial records

maintained by the Houses of bin Laden and Saud

where these families kept stashes of gold, silver and diamonds and who controlled these stashes.

(2) Jamie knew what had to be done to put the House of Saud out of the oil business for at least a couple of years. The oil industry infrastructure was at least as vulnerable as the U.S. fuel and power infrastructures had proven to be.

(3) Jamie had compiled a list of 300 people, mostly members of the Houses of bin Laden and Saud, who he believed had played a direct role in the attacks on the U.S.

He was going to see that they died.

(4) Jamie had also compiled a list of Saudis who he thought might be able to change Saudi Arabia and give its people a better and more democratic future.

(5) Lastly Jamie was going to personally kill the Lord.

Chapter 22- Finding the Lord

During the many months of tracing money Jamie had come to many dead ends. The search was tedious and Jamie often worked 20 hours at a stretch. The House of Saud and the House of bin Laden had thousands of bank accounts with thousands of real and fake companies serving as fronts for these bank accounts. The vast wealth which came from oil came from many directions. It came through oil companies from many countries. It came from thousand of buyers. In some cases the Saudis were paid by cash, sometimes through barter. A certain number of barrels of oil for a certain tonnage of grain. A certain number of barrels for a certain number of weapons. Cash received by the House of Saud went in many directions. It went in and out of thousands of bank accounts to hundreds of thousands of sources. All of the receipts and all of the expenditures were in hundreds of thousands of entries into computer data banks. The reasons for some expenditure were very vague while much money was spent for purposes never stated. It was easier for Jamie to begin his search with the monies spent by those who hijacked the commercial airliners on September 11, 2001 and through the monies spent by Osama bin Laden for his training camps. It was only by accident that Jamie discovered the links between Osama and the Lord. Early in his investigation Jamie had discovered the link between the Lord, as a banker for the House of Saud, and the House of bin Laden. However, the Lord and his bank was only one of the thousands of bankers who handled money for the House of Saud and the House of bin Laden. It was only through luck that Jamie found the PowerPoint presentation which described the attacks planned against the U.S.

Chapter 23-Time for Action

Now it was time for Jamie to carry out his plan. He had prepared a balance sheet gleaned from tens of thousands of financial data bases covering the financial dealings of the Houses of bin Laden and Saud.

He was surprised to see how much the two families owed in

debt to Western banks. Oil revenue came in through Aramco

which was the oil company owned by the House of Saud.

The two families held stocks and bonds and had large sums

of money in banks. In the mid 1990's the two families had

started several Islamic banks based in Oman, Dubai, Yemen,

United Arab Emirates and other Arab nations. Most of the

stocks and bonds they owned were pledged as security for

some of the giant loans the families had made to finance

various projects. As best Jamie could determine the two

families had liquid assets of just fewer than two trillion

dollars. This despite the fact that the two families distributed

huge amounts of money within the two families and despite

enormous subsidies paid to various categories of Saudis.

They also owned stocks and bonds worth as much as 1 and a

half trillion dollars which were pledged for loans made by

Western banks. It was clear

to Jamie that the Saudis were not good managers of money and that Western banks had taken advantage of their lack of financial sophistication.

Jamie wrote a software program which upon his command would transfer all of the liquid wealth of the Saudis to various other non Saudi places. His software program also allowed him to hack into the data banks of the Western banks which held as security the one and half trillion dollars of Saudi securities and release these securities so ownership could be transferred as Jamie saw fit. Through his hacking Jamie would remove from the Western bank balance sheet any interest they had in Saudi securities. This would include eliminating the documentations which had originally confirmed the existence of the loans made to the Saudis by the banks. All that was necessary was for Jamie to send coded instructions and it would all happen.

To eliminate the Saudis from the oil business Jamie had devised a computer program which would use the Saudi Air Force to attack certain key installations. The computer program would order 80 Saudi fighter jets to arm and scramble. Once the jets were airborne the computer program would take over control of the flight path from the pilots and tell them that at a prescribed time they would be ejected from their cockpits. Once each of the aircraft reached their particular targets they would each automatically fire rockets. Crude oil is very volatile and eighty well placed rockets would put the Saudis out of the oil business for at least two years. When Jamie was ready all he had to do is to give the computer the necessary commands. Jamie had prepared a list of Saudis that he was going to kill. He knew where each of these Saudis was at any one time because each had chips surgically placed under their skin with transponders which traced their whereabouts in a computer program to which Jamie had access. He could look on his computer and know where each of his intended victims was at any time of the day or night. The House of Saud had implemented this program as protection against kidnapping.

The last part of Jamie's revenge was to kill the person at the tip of the command pyramid. When Jamie was ready he was going to England to personally kill the Lord.

Chapter 24-The Money

Jamie had chosen September 11th as the day of reckoning. He spent the night of September 10th in his North London home going over his check list. The first item on his list concerned how to rob the House of Saud and the House of bin Laden of their wealth. His years of experience with computers, along with the detailed inside information he possessed regarding the computer systems used by the two rich Saudi families helped him greatly. In addition he had a small team of the best Hackers money could buy working in one of his companies in Finland. He and his team had identified the locations of all the wealth of the Houses of Saud and bin Laden. Some of the wealth was based upon the ownership of land at locations all over the globe. The Saudis had to keep track of what they owned and they did so on the computers programmed by Jamie's company. Jamie and his team compiled a data bank which reflected the location of real estate and the documents which evidenced the ownership of the real estate. To their dismay they determined that much of the real estate owned by the two Saudi families was being used as collateral for large loans extended by banks mostly centered in the Arab countries of Dubai and the United Arab Emirates. Accordingly, most of this wealth was not really wealth since it could not be accessed by the Saudis. It was not liquid wealth. For any monies to be taken from the real estate, the real estate would need to be sold and the underlying debts paid off. In a world recession, which Jamie believed he was about to cause; the real estate of the Saudis might not sell for as much as was owed on it. The Saudis also were hoarding large quantities of gold and silver in several locations within Saudi Arabia. Their computers indicated where these hoards of wealth could be found and who controlled access to them. The next category of wealth of the Saudis were certificates of deposits and other bank deposits at hundreds of banks all over the world. In every instance where a certificate of deposit or bank account exists records would exist in terms of who could access or transfer the monies in these bank accounts. The computers of the various banks reflected this information. Jamie had hacked into and accumulated from the Saudi's computers the access numbers, passwords and codes he would need to transfer these funds to whomever and wherever he wanted. He and his team had developed a complex software program complete with access codes and passwords and upon his command the hundreds of billions of dollars in the Saudi bank accounts would simply disappear from the Saudi accounts and re-appear in accounts created by Jamie. On September 11th

Jamie gave that command and all of sudden the bank accounts of the House of Saud and the House of bin Laden showed zero balances. It was the largest single day transfer of money in history. It was also the largest bank robbery in history.

Chapter 25- The Oil

Hamad's beeper had gone off at 0600 and a message on his cell phone from his squadron commander ordered him to report to his base at Dhahran and be ready to scramble. When he arrived at the base he quickly put on his flight uniform and rode out to his aircraft. As a pilot of a Tornado fighter jet he was among the elite of the Royal Saudi Air Force. He had been trained as a pilot in Italy and Great Britain and he was a good pilot. When he got to his plane he found that his co-pilot / weapons technician was already in the aircraft and ready to go. He noted that the fighter jet had a full tank of fuel and was fully armed with eight 1000 pound bombs. He immediately buckled himself into the aircraft and with instructions from the flight control tower he and his aircraft were soon in the air. He assumed this was all part of a drill and he could see a number of other Tornados from his squadron already in the air or lined up to take off.

Hashim had also received a call on his beeper at 0600 and a coded message telling him to report to his aircraft and be ready to scramble. As a pilot of an F-15C fighter jet he had been trained as a pilot in the United States and while in the United States had met and married a woman from Kansas. He left her in a warm bed to head to his base at Dhahran. At the base he quickly dressed in his flight suit and headed to his aircraft. His only instructions came from a computerized message telling him to scramble. His plane was fully fueled and armed with AIM-7F/M Sparrow missiles for use in air to air combat. As he taxied to take off he could see that his entire squadron was being scrambled for some sort of training mission.

Many miles southwest of the air base at Dhahran at Khamis Mushayt, Fahd and Bakri had received messages to report to the base for duty in their aircraft. Fahd's fighter was also a Tornado while Bakri was the pilot of a F-15. They were also soon in the air with their squadron.

The primary mission of the Royal Saudi Air Force is to protect the country from foreign attack from any of its' neighbors. However, most of the world knew that the primary protection of the kingdom came from the United States. Now, however, the United States, because of the disastrous attacks on it would be unable to protect the kingdom from it's' enemies. By 0730 the Royal Saudi Air Force had sixty Tornados and forty F-15 C's in the air over the kingdom. The primary duty of the Royal Saudi Air Force this morning was to protect the capacity of the House of Saud to produce oil. It was oil that gave the family its' wealth. In addition to fighter jets the oil fields, refineries and storage depots scattered across the kingdom were protected by SAM air defense systems. Like most weapons systems the SAMs around key portions of the Saudi oil infrastructure were controlled by computer software systems which in turn were meant to be controlled by technicians in underground control stations. However, on this morning these weapons systems were controlled by a software program designed by one of Jamie's technicians in Finland. At 0740 all of the SAM missiles surrounding oil installations in Saudi Arabia fired into the air and came rebounding back to the ground to damage the installations they were designed to protect. At 0745 the Tornado and F-15C pilots lost the ability to fly their fighters. Instead their fighters were being flown by a computer program designed by one of Jamie's technicians. The pilots and crews found that they could not radio ground control. Ground control crews remained blissfully unaware that an alien force had seized all

one hundred of the airborne fighter aircraft. At 0750 the

canopies of the Tornadoes and F-15 C's separated from each

aircraft and the crews were ejected into the air. The pilots

and crew members gently floated towards the ground all over

the kingdom. However, their aircraft remained in the air.

Ten of the Tornadoes proceeded to the Abqaiq complex, the

world's largest oil-processing facility. Beginning at 0815

each of the aircraft made bombing runs on the complex

dropping a total of eighty 1000 pound bombs. After

dropping their bombs the aircraft proceeded to head straight

into what was left of the complex to bring additional damage

to the complex. By 0845 the complex was completely

destroyed and flames shot hundreds of feet into the air fueled

by Saudi light crude.

Also beginning at 0815 ten more Tornadoes began bombing

runs at oil loading terminals at Ras Tanura and Ju'aymah, on

Saudi Arabia's east coast. These computer guided aircraft struck the facility at Ras Tanura known as "Sea Island" which along with Ju'aymah would normally move as many as nine million barrels of oil per day. This vast amount of oil provided a huge amount of fuel for the eighty 1000 pound bombs dropped on the facilities. The remaining Tornados and their bombs hit pumping stations all over the Kingdom. The forty

F-15C's and their weaponry hit the buildings which contained the Managers who maintained and managed the oil infrastructure of Saudi Arabia.

The production of oil by the Kingdom of Saudi Arabia which gave the Houses of Saud and bin Laden the money they needed to finance their Jihad against the United States was now gone. The security which was designed to protect the infrastructure which produced the oil had been used to destroy it. Jamie had destroyed the Saudis capability to produce oil by using the military power of the Royal Saudi Air Force. The backbone of the Royal Saudi Air Force was the Tornando IDS fighter jet. The aircraft was originally developed by an international team composed of the UK's British Aerospace, Germanys MBB and Italy's Aeritalia. The Saudis had spent large sums of money to purchase 96 of these planes in 1993. Pilot training was provided by the Royal Air Force of Great Britain and by the U.S. Air Force. Although the Tornando has been in production for more than 30 years it still provided one of the highest weapons payload weight to empty weight of any aircraft ever built except for the more advanced F-16. Each of the Tornandos carries a pilot and a weapons' officer. Like most modern aircraft the aircraft and its' weapons system is guided and / or operated by computers. Computer systems monitor takeoffs, flights, landings and the launching of weapons. The aircrafts most potent weapon is an air to air missile, the AIM-9 Sidewinder. Jamie had used these aircraft to destroy the Saudi's capacity to pump, refine and transport oil. The destruction he had caused would put the Saudis out of the oil business for years and make it unlikely that they would be able to ever again attain the wealth they had previously enjoyed. His computer programs had allowed him to seize control of the most potent portion of the Royal Saudi Air Force. Once the aircraft were airborne Jamie's computer program seized control of the planes and left the pilots unable to control the plane or use its' weapon systems. The pilots were unable to radio each other or ground command. After their controls were seized the pilot and weapons technician were automatically ejected from the plane. Jamie only needed to give the computer the commands. On September 11th he gave that command.

Chapter 26- The House of Saud and the House of Bin Laden

Jamie had spent thousands of hours identifying who in the Houses of Saud and bin Laden had planned, financed or carried out the plans to carry out the attacks on the United States. His list also included those who had helped plan, helped finance or helped carry out the attacks on the United States in any way. His list did not include those who simply cheered the attacks on the U.S. That would have required the murders of more than a million Saudis and the murders of hundreds of millions of other people in other nations. The United States had few friends and lots of enemies in the world. Jamie's list began with the Saudi King and most of the House of Saud members who held various posts in the Saudi government. It also included most of the members of the family council, the Council of Fifty,whose approval the Saudi King needed to stay in power. The list also included many clerics who made the focus of their lives the destruction of all those who could not be converted to Wahhabism.

The list also included many members of the House of bin Laden who had helped the House of Saud advance the goals of the Jihad against the people of the United States. Jamie's task in locating those he wanted to kill was aided by the way the House of Saud kept up with members of the family. The House of Saud worried about kidnapping and so every member of the House of Saud had been implanted with a computer chip tied into a global positioning satellite. This implant made it possible for the family to know exactly where a family member was at any time. The system would give the exact location. Jamie's team had developed hundreds of drones containing a deadly poison. The drones were controlled by radio signals send from a satellite in space. Each drone was programmed to follow the coordinates provided by the embedded computer chip. The drones were programmed to go through open windows or doors if the target was inside. If no door or window was open the drone was programmed to hover until the target was available. All 300 drones were programmed to be launched from a trawler anchored in the Red Sea. Each was about the size of a sea gull and in flight each looked like a sea gull. They would all be launched within a half hour time span upon a computer command signal issued by Jamie. On September 11th Jamie issued that command.

Chapter 27-The Lord's Last Flight

Jamie was going to kill the Lord himself. He had studied the Lord's habits carefully and knew that the Lord took an early morning walk in St James Park each weekday morning at 6 a.m. Some mornings were foggy and cold but regardless of the weather the Lord always took his early morning walk. The Lord felt no need to take a bodyguard with him during his walks. As a Lord he felt supremely safe in St. James Park.

On the morning of September 11th after issuing computer commands which had zeroed out the balances of thousands of Saudi bank accounts, launched fighter jets to destroy the capabilities of the Saudis to produce oil and launched more than 300 drones to quietly poison more than 300 Saudis, Jamie rode in the front seat of a small van. It was 5:45 a.m. and Jamie knew that at a few minutes past 6 a.m. the Lord would be walking through a part of St. James Park which was out of sight of security cameras and out of sight of the general public. The Lord felt no need to protect himself from kidnapping. After all he was a Lord and this was his country and he had taken this walk every morning for more than ten years. With Jamie were two large Men who had worked for Jamie for many years. One was his cousin Joe from Tennessee and the other was his friend Billy from Memphis. As the Lord reached the side of the van the two men quickly grabbed him and covered his mouth to keep him from screaming. They covered his nose with ether and trussed him up with rope in the back of the van. They were unseen as they accomplished this task. Jamie drove the van to a small airport in North London. At the airport the men loaded the Lord into a small aircraft and securely handcuffed him in a small cage on the inside of the aircraft. The cage would allow the Lord to see where he was but he could not loosen himself from the cage. The Lord began to awaken in his little cage at about 8 a.m. Jamie was sitting in a seat next to his cage. Jamie introduced himself. He told the Lord who he was and why he was there. In a quiet and calm voice tinged with anger Jamie told the Lord about his wife, daughter, son and his grand children. He told the Lord that they had a right to live. He told him that they had been in a plane in Chicago when the dirty bomb exploded. He did not need to tell the Lord more about why he was there. Jamie told the Lord that in a few minutes the plane would take off by remote control. He said the back of the plane was loaded with highly combustible fuel. He said that the plane would be in the air for less than an hour. At 8:45 a.m. the airplane would hit one of the white cliffs near Dover which overlook the English Channel. The only pain the Lord would suffer would be the anxiety he would experience during the 45 minute flight. Once the plane hit the cliff he would be vaporized. The head of the largest bank in England didn't show up for work that morning. He was never seen again and his disappearance would remain a mystery forever.

Epilogue-

The events of this anniversary of the September 11th attacks on the U.S. had repercussions far beyond what Jamie had expected. The first and immediate effect is that the world spot market for crude oil soared to more than $90.00 a barrel. The crude oil crisis had immediate effects in the U.S. The U.S. was slowly recovering from the massive attacks which had deprived the country of fuel and power. The economy was in tatters. Many businesses had failed and many Americans had fled the country. Both Canada and Mexico placed tight restrictions on entry into their countries. The U.S. rapidly enacted laws forcing Americans to reduce their dependence upon fossil fuel. Huge surcharges were placed upon large personal vehicles. Many city centers were placed off limits to personal vehicles forcing people to get to work by public transit. The money which Jamie had taken from the Saudis and transferred to his accounts and to those of his five friends left him in control of the largest fortune ever accumulated by one man.

After September 11th Jamie spent a month destroying all links which any one could use to find him and to discover who was behind the events of September 11th. Saudi Arabia was now what it had been before 1938. A poor nation with limited income. The more than five million workers who had lived and worked in Saudi Arabia went back to their home countries. The House of Saud was not strong enough to continue to rule Saudi Arabia as a royal family. The Kingdom was gone forever. Jamie had also deleted all the information in all the computer data bases in all of the computers in the computer networks of the House of Saud and the House of bin Laden. That made it impossible for surviving members of the House of Saud or the House of bin Laden to locate any of the families lost wealth. Jamie also sent in specially trained teams to remove the gold, silver and diamonds kept by the members of the House of Saud who had been killed. A number of Saudis who had lived as expatriates returned to the country and established a new government. They were helped by large sums of money which had mysteriously appeared in the account of one Expatriate group in London. After covering his tracks Jamie left London and went back to Illinois. In Illinois he turned over his house to his cousin who was now too old to farm the land which surrounded the house. The cousin's son moved into the smaller house and took over the job of farming the land. Jamie converted much of his wealth into something easy to carry and something easy to use. He left the United States in a small private jet carrying a large fortune in precious jewels. He also retained access to hundreds of bank accounts containing money which had once been in the accounts of the Houses of Saud and bin Laden. He had also turned his companies over to the members of his team.

The events that Jamie had caused to feed and satisfy his rage caused him to reflect on what he had done. With the huge amount of money he had accumulated he thought perhaps he could go after other evil doers in other parts of the world. There was no shortage of evil in the world and for a few days Jamie contemplated spending the rest of his days attacking and destroying evil as he had done with the Lord, the House of Saud and the House of bin Laden. However, after some thought he decided that he would leave the fight against evil to others. He thought he had done his part and, in fact, he had only sought to feed his Rage and avenge the deaths of his family. He would have traded every penny he had if he could only one more time look into the eyes of Donna and hear her voice. If he could kiss her lips one more time.

The events created by Jamie had an enormous effect on the world. It limited the possibility that there would be more attacks on the United States. The attacks on the U.S. had effectively removed the United States as a world power. .

. . .

. .

www.ingramcontent.com/pod-product-compliance
Lightning Source LLC
Chambersburg PA
CBHW071331280526
45787CB00001B/62